VEGETABLES · ON THE · GRILL

by Kelly McCune

Design by
Thomas Ingalls

Produced by
David Barich

Photography by
Deborah Jones

Food Styling by
Sandra Cook

HarperPerennial
A Division of HarperCollins*Publishers*

Acknowledgements

A big thanks to Mira Velimirovic for recipe development and her terrific test kitchen. Thank you to Suzanne Gottschang for her excellent suggestions.

Vegetables on the Grill
Copyright © 1992 by The Grill Group

HarperCollins, Publishers, Inc.
10 East 53rd Street
New York, NY 10022

Book and Cover Design:
Ingalls + Associates
Design: Thomas Ingalls and Harumi H. Kubo

Photography and Set Design:
Deborah Jones

Food Styling and Props:
Sandra Cook

Prop Stylist:
Sara Slavin

Assistant to the Photographer:
Melissa Hawkins

Backgrounds:
Missy Hamilton

Editing:
Frances Bowles

Library of Congress Cataloging-in-Publication Data

McCune, Kelly.
    Vegetables on the grill / by Kelly McCune ; design
by Thomas Ingalls ; produced by David Barich ;
photography by Deborah Jones ; food styling by
Sandra Cook.
        p.   cm.
    Includes index.
    ISBN 0-06-096889-3
    1. Barbecue cookery. 2. Vegetarian cookery.
I. Ingalls, Thomas. II. Barich, David. III. Jones,
Deborah. IV. Cook, Sandra. V. Title.
TX840.B3M433 1992
641.5′784—dc20   91-58458
                                                            CIP

Printed in Japan

92 93 94 10 9 8 7 6 5 4 3 2

For Isabel, my little vegetable-lover.

Contents

Introduction   8

Chapter I   11   **Tools, Techniques, and Marinades**

Chapter II   23   **A Glossary of Vegetarian Foods for the Grill**

Chapter III   41   **Hot Off the Grill**

43   Polenta with Green Chili and Red Pepper

44   Coconut, Lime, and Ginger-marinated Vegetables

46   Roasted Acorn Squash with Wild Rice Salad

49   Sandwich Grill

50   Skewered Vegetables with Cilantro Sauce

53   Yams, Apples, and Leeks with Spicy Pecan Nut Butter

54   Fresh Figs and Vegetables with Couscous

57   Baby Vegetables with Pasta and Fresh Herb Sauce

58   Root Vegetables with Warm Mustard Greens Sauce

61   Skewered Tofu, Mushrooms, Daikon, and Bok Choy

62   Grilled Appetizers

65   Corn Bread–stuffed Peppers with Chipotle Sauce

66   Middle Eastern Eggplant Sandwich with Tahini Dressing

69   Vegetable Medley with Three Dipping Sauces

70   Summer Salad with Quinoa

73   Corn Cakes with Roasted Vegetables

74   Vegetables with Northern Indian Almond-Spice Sauce

76   Garlicky Portobello Mushrooms

79   Basil and Pine Nut Polenta with Salsa Cruda

81   Grilled Tempeh with Red Onion and Eggplant on Toast

83   Eggplant, New Potato, and Fennel with Sour Cream Sauce

85   Tofu Satay with Tangy Dipping Sauce

86   Grill Cocktail Party

88   Wood-smoked Pizzas

Tools and Fuels Sources   91

***Grill Book* List of Menus**   92

***The Art of Grilling* List of Menus**   92

Index   93

I come to the writing of this book not as a vegetarian, but as someone seeking an approach to cooking with less emphasis on meat, more focus on interesting and delicious nonmeat dishes. Grilling usually conjures up images of sizzling beefsteaks, barbecued chicken, and hamburgers. These are wonderful, traditional grill foods, but I found I wanted more ways to cook and combine vegetables and to put them at the *center* of the meal. I was also prompted by more and more requests for recipes that did not include meat. Grilling, after all, is not for carnivores only! ¶ ***Grill Book*** (1986), and ***The Art of Grilling*** (1990) are devoted to a healthful, delicious way of cooking on the grill. In those books vegetables get some attention—as wonderful grilled side dishes. In only a few of the menus are vegetables or tofu the center of the meal. With the increased awareness of the high fat and cholesterol contents of meats, and the connection between an over-consumption of them and health problems, more people are looking for new and exciting ways to cook and eat vegetables. Many people have given up red meat altogether; others are cutting back dramatically. ¶ We Americans tend to focus the meal on a large meat dish and augment it with vegetables, pasta, or rice. A meatless meal may not have a discernable "center"—it may have more components, more ingredients, or the dishes may be of equal importance. While the recipes may seem to be more labor intensive, the reward is in the flavor, the complexity, and the wholesomeness. Cooking for a vegetarian diet requires an approach that considers all the components equally. Though this may be a new way of thinking, it is timely. ¶ Vegetables have a delightful texture and lose none of their flavor on the grill. Because of their slight sugar content, the outside browns and seals quickly, locking in flavor and moisture. ***Vegetables on the Grill*** also includes recipes for grilling tofu, breads, and polenta. These make delicious accompaniments to grilled vegetables and serve to round out the meal. In **Grill Book** I gave basic grilling methods for 22 different vegetables and fruits. By contrast, the Glossary of Vegetarian Foods in *Vegetables on the Grill* describes how to grill over 60 vegetables, fruits, and nonmeat foods. The first chapter gives techniques and tips specific to the grilling of vegetables and contains recipes for marinades, bastes, and oils. ¶ The dishes in *Vegetables on the Grill* make hearty, satisfying fare. The flavors range in influence from the foods of Italy, California, and New Mexico, to Thailand, Japan, and the Middle East. Roasted Acorn Squash with Wild Rice Salad draws on distinctly American cooking, but the squash is roasted on the grill rather than in the oven, with a delicious charcoal-smoked flavor as the result. Polenta is borrowed from Italy and mixed with green chilies and red peppers to give it a Southwest flavor, and the Thai dish, *satay,* is made with tofu strips rather than the traditional beef or chicken. The grilled pizzas, subtly flavored with wood smoke, will please any palate. ¶ I used a kettle-shaped grill and mesquite charcoal when creating these recipes, so the cooking times should be considered as guidelines rather than exact measures if you are using anything else. The grill should be tended and the food checked for doneness periodically for the most successful results. If you are cooking with fuel other than mesquite charcoal (including gas), the food may require longer cooking time; mesquite burns hotter than briquets and gas grills set at low. ¶ Cooking food on a charcoal grill is a delightful experience and always gives food a delicious smoky flavor that cannot be duplicated by any other method. This book demonstrates a world of new grilling possibilities for both the vegetarian and the health-conscious eater. Above all, grilling is a time to be outdoors, to relax and enjoy the crackling fire and the aromas and the taste of good food cooked over the coals.

CHAPTER 1

Tools, Techniques, and Marinades

Cooking vegetables over the dry heat of a charcoal grill fire gives them a smoky, savory flavor while heightening their natural sweetness. The hot coals quickly seal the outside of the vegetables, allowing the inside flesh to cook in its own moisture. The result is a different but more complex flavor than that of vegetables cooked by boiling or steaming. In addition, grilling seals in vitamins and minerals that might otherwise be cooked away. Some vegetables are simply so delicious grilled you won't consider cooking them any other way.

This chapter primarily addresses the question of how to cook vegetables on the grill; however, unless otherwise noted nearly all the tips on fire preparation, special tools, and cooking techniques can be applied to fruits and other foods such as tofu and tempeh. Chapter 2, A Glossary of Vegetarian Foods for the Grill, gives specific cooking times and techniques.

About Grilling Vegetables

Most vegetables cook beautifully on the grill with just a minimum of preparation or attention. As is true when grilling anything, the most important skill to be mastered is patience: Allow the coals to burn long enough to be covered by gray ash, otherwise the fire will be too hot and the vegetables will burn. Vegetables contain a fair amount of natural sugar, which is why they are sealed quickly and acquire a light crust when cooked by a dry heat method. But it is this sugar content that will cause them to burn if the fire is too hot. Fruit, which contains even more sugar, will require an even lower fire—coals still more thickly coated with gray ash.

Unless the peel is thick and woody, fibrous, or tough, most vegetables will not need to be peeled. If they are relatively small, vegetables are delicious cooked whole, but are also easy and quick to cook when sliced or cut into chunks first. A good standard slice thickness is between one-third and one-half inch. Bite-sized chunks (three-quarter-inch cubes) are the easiest to skewer.

The cooking grid should be lightly oiled to prevent sticking, and the vegetables will brown more evenly when lightly brushed with oil. Olive oil and other vegetable oils burn at a very high temperature and are thus good choices for brushing on foods to be grilled. Nut oils are delicate and burn at low temperatures. They should be used carefully since they will give food a burned and bitter taste if the fire is too hot. Some vegetables do not need any oil, a point that is specifically noted in the relevant glossary listings.

If your grill is large enough to accommodate it, build a fire that has a cooler spot and a hotter spot. This allows you to sear the vegetables over the hotter coals and move them to a less intense part of the grill to finish cooking. On a gas grill, preheat one side and turn it off for the cool side; leave the other burner on low for the hot side. As a

general rule, most vegetables require a total cooking time of between 15 and 20 minutes and cook more evenly on a covered grill. Testing doneness with a wooden skewer is a very reliable method—if the vegetable is tender when pierced with the skewer, it is likely to be done.

Vegetables, whether sliced or whole, can be grilled right on the cooking grid but can also be threaded onto metal or wooden skewers, or arranged in a hinged grill basket. Some vegetables are too small and delicate to be grilled directly over the fire; these can be wrapped in foil, but pierce the foil with holes to allow smoke to penetrate the packet and flavor the food.

Open Grilling is cooking without a hood or top over the grill. The coals tend to remain hotter when the hood is up or off, because the draft around them is increased. Food browns quickly and therefore needs to be somewhat thinly sliced so that it cooks through in a short time before overbrowning. Open grilling is not recommended for whole vegetables. If skewered, the vegetables should be sliced into bite-sized chunks.

Covered Grilling is cooking with the hood down over the grill. This technique allows you more control of the fire as the vents can be used to regulate the draft. A hood on the grill gives you more versatility, since the vegetables can be browned and also roasted inside the hot covered grill. Whole vegetables require covered grilling.

Lighting a Charcoal Fire

Vegetables and fruit have delicate flavors and textures than can be easily marred by the chemical taste of some charcoal starters. In particular lighter fluid, which never completely burns away, gives off a strong-smelling smoke than can be absorbed by the food and give it an acrid taste. Starter-impregnated charcoal briquets are also guilty of masking the fresh flavor of grilled vegetables. Starters have been shown to harm the environment by adding considerable volumes of pollutants to the air, an effect serious enough that in Southern California these products are regulated. So it's best to use one of the simple mechanical fire-starting techniques. I strongly recommend your making an investment in a charcoal chimney starter or an electric coil starter, or collecting kindling to light the grill. The chimney and the electric starter are predictable, always on hand once you've made the initial purchase, and are safe and wonderfully simple to use.

Charcoal Chimney Starter: Like an oversized coffee can, which is what it originally was, the charcoal chimney starter is little more than a metal cylinder, though the ones sold in the supermarket and gourmet stores have a shielded handle, a shelf for the coals, and perforations to allow a draft. The chimney starter is the easiest and most reliable method of lighting coals. It lights them all at once and therefore evenly, no chemicals are needed, and because of the intense heat built up inside the chimney, the coals light faster than they do with lighter fluid. If kept out of the rain and damp, a chimney starter will last several years, making it a good investment.

Pile the coals into the top portion of the starter and place a crumpled sheet of newspaper in the bottom. Place the chimney on the fuel grate and light the paper. Add another crumpled sheet if needed after 2 or 3 minutes. When the coals at the top are alight and the flaming has subsided, dump them onto the fuel grate and arrange, if needed, with long-handled tongs. Place the hot chimney starter in a safe place until it has cooled. Allow the coals to burn down enough to become covered with ash so that there is no black showing. A properly burned-down fire will take about 40 minutes from when it is first lit until it is ready to be used.

Chimney starters make it easy to light extra coals for the grill: Load the chimney as usual, place it on a fireproof surface, and ignite it. When the coals are lit and the flaming has subsided, either dump them onto the fuel grate or place them in the grill with long-handled tongs.

Electric Coil Starter: Nestle the oval heating element of an electric coil starter among the coals piled on the fuel grate. Plug it in and, in about 10 minutes, the coals it touches will begin flaming. Then, with long-handled tongs, you will need to arrange the unlit coals so that they touch the lit ones and wait until the coals burn down enough to be ash covered. This procedure, too, takes about 40 minutes.

Kindling: To start a fire with kingling, roll a sheet of newspaper on the diagonal and twist it into a loose pretzel-shaped knot. Make 2 more of these "pretzels" and place them on the fuel grate. Arrange dry twigs on top of the newspaper and coals on top of the twigs. Light the paper. The coals will be ready in about 40 minutes.

Lighter Fluid: The use of lighter fluid is the most popular method of lighting a charcoal fire but may be seeing its last days. It pollutes the air (in Southern California it has been stringently regulated, and residents are learning other ways to light the coals) and gives food a chemical taste if not allowed to burn off *completely*. It is also dangerous, particularly when squirted directly onto flaming coals—a common error in judgment. All things considered, it is best to learn one of the mechanical methods, which are reliable, inexpensive, and safe.

Solid Starters: Solid starters are usually made from wood chips and paraffin wax pressed into a block. The small blocks are placed on the fuel grate, the coals are spread on top, and the starters are ignited. They are slow and tend to light only the coals they are touching. They are, however, safe and easy.

When the Fire is Ready

A charcoal fire requires between 30 and 45 minutes to reach the proper temperature for cooking. For a hotter fire once the coals are ready, push the coals together and open all the vents. For a less intense fire, spread the coals out and control the temperature by partially closing the vents.

Red-hot coals: When the coals are red hot, a red glow is visible through a light coating of white ash. You will be able to hold your palm at a distance of about 6 inches from the fire for only 3 or 4 seconds. This temperature is best for searing.

Medium-hot coals: When the coals are medium hot, the coating of grayish white ash will be thicker and the red glow nearly invisible. You can hold your palm over the fire for up to 6 seconds now. This is the best temperature for grilling most vegetables, with the hood on or off.

Low coals: When the heat of the coals is low, the coating of gray ash is quite thick, and you can hold your palm over the fire for 10 seconds. This is best for slow cooking on a covered grill.

Extended fire: To create a fire that will last an hour or more, light one batch of coals. When they are just getting ash covered, add more coals and allow those to burn down until they, too, are ash covered. This type of fire will take over 45 minutes, but will save you time since it makes a longer-lasting fire from the outset.

Special Tools for Vegetable Grilling

Aluminum Foil: Heavy-duty aluminum foil can be used in a number of ways on the grill. Laid flat on the cooking grid, pierced all over with holes, and lightly oiled, it makes a great surface for cooking delicate or small vegetables or fruits that might otherwise fall into the fire. You can also place the food on the center of a sheet, fold the sheet into a packet, pierce it all over with holes, and place it on the cooking grid. You should turn these packets occasionally to keep the food inside from burning. Holes poked in the foil let the grill smoke in to flavor the food, which is the point of cooking over a charcoal fire in the first place. If you make an entirely sealed packet, none of that smoke flavor can penetrate it.

Crumple aluminum foil and use it as an improvised brush for scraping off the cooking grid. Take care to hold it with a mitt on a hot grill since aluminum is a great conductor of heat.

Create small aluminum baking cups in which to roast garlic and shallots on top of the grill.

Basting Brushes: Brushes are indispensable for basting on oil, marinades, or sauces. Choose the well-made, long-handled varieties and invest in several. Reserve one for brushing oil onto the cooking grid.

Griffo Grill: The Griffo Grill, a relatively new product, is a modified top designed so that smaller foods can be grilled. It is a heavy-gauge enameled steel sheet with cut-out holes small enough so that food won't fall through. The sheet is placed directly on the cooking grid. It comes in a rectangular shape, square, or curved on one side to fit a kettle-style grill.

Hinged Wire Grill Baskets: Two heavy wire racks hinged together hold the food in place in these "baskets" for the grill. The flat basket is placed directly on the cooking rack and, with its long handle, it is easy and safe to turn and remove. They come in a variety of shapes and sizes—look for the ones with long handles. Oil the inside of the basket before cooking to keep food from sticking.

Marinade Pans: Foods can be marinated in any type of bowl, baking dish, or pan, whether made of glass, porcelain, or stainless steel. You can even use the shiny, disposable, aluminum baking tins. The substance to avoid is uncoated aluminum (some jellyroll pans, baking pans, and cookie sheets are made of this) since it can react with the acid in the marinade and give food an off taste.

Vegetables on the Grill

Mitts: At least one good heavy mitt is essential when grilling, to be used for handling hot metal skewers, tongs, cooking racks, vents, or any other potentially hot grill equipment.

Skewers: Wooden skewers are great for grilling quick-cooking foods on the grill. Soak them first in water for 15 minutes or more to keep them from burning up too quickly on the grill. For longer cooking times, metal skewers are needed. Metal skewers conduct heat and cook vegetables on the inside, so they are useful for dense root vegetables. The notched, flat, or twisted kinds are best since food is less likely to spin around when being turned.

Spatulas or Turners: Long-handled spatulas are safest, since your hand can be well away from the hot fire. Wide-bladed spatulas are handy for turning large items on the grill.

Tongs: Choose long-handled, spring-loaded tongs, which can be easily manipulated when you are wearing a mitt. One set of tongs can be specially reserved for moving coals.

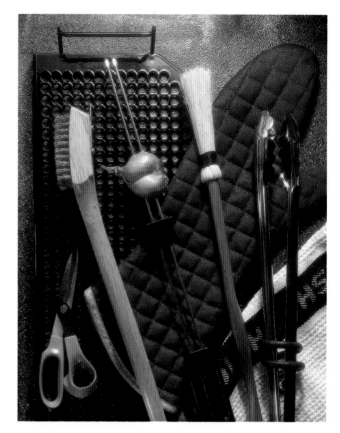

A Glossary of Grilling Tips and Techniques

Charcoal: Many different charcoals are available in the market today. *Briquets* are the most widely sold, though they don't burn as hot or as clean as hardwood charcoal does. Avoid briquets that contain starter additives or raw coal, both of which can give the food a chemical taste. Allow briquets to burn long enough to acquire a coating of ash. *Mesquite charcoal* is becoming more widely available in the supermarkets. It is a variety of hardwood charcoal made from burning mesquite wood slowly until it is completely carbonized. Because it has no binders or fillers as briquets do, it burns cleaner and a bit hotter. It also snaps and pops, so stand clear while it ignites. The pieces remaining after the fire is extinguished can be reused. Mesquite *charcoal* burns hot and clean and gives very little smoky flavor to food; mesquite *wood,* however, imparts such a strong smoky wood flavor that most vegetables may be overwhelmed. *Hardwood charcoal,* like mesquite charcoal, is made directly from wood pieces. It does add a smokier flavor to food and, like mesquite, burns hotter than briquets do and very clean. It can also be reused. It is, however, more difficult to find hardwood charcoal. *Hardwood briquets* are new to the market. These briquets, un-like the others, are made from noncarbonized wood pulp pressed into a briquet. They smoke considerably when igniting and do not last as long as briquets. *Hardwood* can be ignited, burned down to glowing embers, and used for cooking. This procedure requires more time than charcoal (up to 1 hour), but it gives food a very distinct smoky flavor, and the fire lasts longer. More wood can be added without the need to light it separately. The best woods are hickory, maple, ash, alder, oak, mesquite, cherry, apple, or the nut woods. Do not use resinous woods such as pine, spruce, or cedar, since they contain pitch which can give food an unpleasant taste. Do not use plywood or lumber of any kind. And do not use any wood you cannot identify.

Charcoal, adding to fire: If your fire is to last beyond 1 hour, you will most likely need to add charcoal. To avoid flavoring the food with the burn-off from igniting coals, light them outside the grill before adding them. This can easily be done on a fireproof surface with a charcoal chimney starter. Mesquite charcoal and hardwood charcoal may be added directly to the fire (they have no additives), but any crackling or spitting as they ignite may cause pieces of charcoal to land on the food.

Charcoal, storage: To guarantee that your fire will start successfully and your grilling be free of anxiety, invest in a large garbage can or bin with a tight-fitting lid in which to store the charcoal. Nothing is more difficult to light than damp charcoal. Coals that won't ever light is the most common grilling disaster, but one that can be avoided.

Cleaning the Grill: Keep the cooking rack clean and well seasoned. The objective should be to have gleaming metal wires, *not* black char-laden ones. This black char does not add flavor and it promotes sticking. If you remember to do so, scrape the cooking rack just after cooking on it, before it has cooled down completely. If you miss this opportunity, scrub it before you light the grill, and again after it has preheated over the hot fire. Wire grill brushes, available in most hardware stores and barbecue stores, are good tools for this most essential task.

Controlling the Heat: The vents are the primary heat control on the grill. Open, they allow more air to circulate around the coals and thus make them hotter; closed, they block the air and lower the temperature of the fire. Bottom vents offer the most direct control over the coals, though the hood vents are also important in controlling heat inside the grill. When the coals are close together, the heat is more intense. Move them apart for a more moderate fire.

Doneness: The variables to consider when determining cooking times are outside temperature (the hotter the day, the faster the cooking time), windiness, and humidity. The temperature of the food before you cook it can also make a difference—for even cooking, bring food to room temperature before grilling. Test doneness with a wooden skewer for the most accurate judgment (unless you want to do a taste test!). If it is tender when pierced with a skewer and browned to your liking, it is most likely done.

Extinguishing the Grill: The simplest way to shut down the grill is to close all the vents and place the hood snugly on top. The lack of oxygen inside will snuff the coals. Avoid dousing the grill with water, since some coals are reusable, and moisture will rust the inside of the grill. Hot coals in an open grill will need to be doused with a heavy layer of ash or with water. Be sure to check any grill after half an hour to be certain that the fire is out.

Flare-ups: Flare-ups commonly occur when you begin cooking before the coals have burned down to an appropriate cooking temperature. Allow the coals to acquire a coating of ash and make certain the flaming has subsided before putting food on the grill. Placing the hood on the grill will usually extinguish flare-ups, as will partially closing the vents. Move the drippy food to a cooler side of the grill, if necessary, or remove it until the fire has burned down some. Avoid the spray gun, since it tends to extinguish the coals and send up clumps of soggy ash.

Flavoring the Fire: Wood chips and chunks can add interesting smoky flavors to foods. In general, moist chips are used for short cooking times and light flavoring; chunks are for long cooking and intense flavor. For a lighter smoky flavor, dry hardwood chunks can be lit with the regular charcoal. Soak wood chips and chunks in water for half an hour before adding them to the fire. This will make them smoke longer and the moisture will help the flavor to penetrate the food. Place wood chips and chunks directly on the hot coals, just before cooking. Take care not to smother the fire with the damp chips. You can always add more after the first handful has burned off. Do not use resinous woods or plant clippings you can't identify. The safest bet is to use wood or herb branches you've grown and dried, or to purchase those packaged specifically for grilling.

The most common woods used for adding smoke flavor are hickory, mesquite, alder, nut woods, oak, olive wood, grapevine, and fruit woods. You can also use herb sprigs, which are most effective when placed directly against the food (on top of the cooking rack). Heavier branched herbs (rosemary or twiggy thyme) may be added to the fire. Orange and lemon peels may be thrown onto the fire for a very light citrus smoke flavor. For the most effect, cover the grill when smoke-flavoring the food.

Marinades, Bastes, Oils, and Sauces

Vegetables can be marinated with delicious results. Many of the more fibrous vegetables take on the subtle flavor of the marinade, fruits can be transformed by an interesting sweet marinade, and certainly tempeh and tofu get their very identity from whatever flavors them.

The following recipes are for basic marinades, bastes, and oils that work well with vegetarian foods for the grill. They are meant as basic palettes to which flavor and color can be added. Marinate most vegetables for 30 minutes at room temperature, or 1 hour in the refrigerator. Any longer will make them mushy. The acidic element in these marinades is used as a flavor booster rather than a tenderizer, since most vegetables do not have tough fibers that need breaking down. Vegetables can marinate in bastes and oils, or these can be brushed on just before grilling. Use these marinades to augment the basic grilling methods outlined for each vegetable described in Chapter 2, A Glossary of Vegetarian Foods for the Grill.

White Wine Marinade   1 cup

This basic wine marinade can be used for most vegetables. Use half the oil for fruit. It is not recommended for tofu or tempeh.

> ¾ cup good white wine
> ⅓ cup olive oil
> ½ a small onion, sliced into rings
> Several large pieces fresh lemon or orange peel
> 1 heaping tablespoon chopped fresh herbs,
>   such as tarragon, basil, sage, oregano, or
>   marjoram, or 1 teaspoon dried herbs
> Several parsley sprigs
> Several grindings fresh black pepper

Combine all the ingredients. Marinate vegetables for 30 minutes at room temperature, or 1 hour in the refrigerator.

Asian Flavors Marinade   1 cup

This recipe suggests a variety of ingredients that can be used in different proportions or in alternate combinations. The dark sesame oil has a pronounced flavor that lasts through grilling, so calculate its use. Soy sauce is salty but infuses vegetables, tofu, and tempeh with flavor. You can substitute tamari for an even fuller soy taste. Peanut oil adds a nutty flavor—a nice balance to the smoky flavor of sesame oil. Ginger and garlic are pungent and penetrate the food, adding lots of good taste.

> ½ cup freshly squeezed orange juice
> 2 tablespoons rice vinegar
> 3 tablespoons soy sauce
> 3 tablespoons peanut oil
> 1 teaspoon dark sesame oil
> 2 large garlic cloves, sliced into ovals
> 1 tablespoon chopped fresh ginger

> 1 green onion, white part and half the green,
>   chopped
> Several sprigs fresh cilantro
> ½ a small dried red chili, minced (optional)

Combine all the ingredients and whisk to emulsify. Marinate vegetables, tofu, or tempeh for 30 minutes at room temperature, or 1 hour in the refrigerator.

Tangy Mustard Marinade   1 cup

Mustard has a delicious bite that blends well with a grilled flavor. This marinade is particularly good on root vegetables, but adds a wonderful dimension to all grilled vegetables.

> 3 tablespoons Dijon-style mustard
> 3 tablespoons grainy mustard
> 3 tablespoons rice vinegar or cider vinegar
> 3 tablespoons olive oil
> 3 tablespoons unfiltered apple juice
> 1 green onion, white part and half the green,
>   minced
> 1 tablespoon chopped fresh sage leaves, or
>   1 teaspoon dried sage
> Plenty of freshly ground black pepper

Combine all the ingredients. Marinate vegetables for 30 minutes at room temperature, or 1 hour in the refrigerator.

Italian Flavors Marinade   ¾ cup

The distinctive smoky flavor of balsamic vinegar is what makes this marinade a great choice for root vegetables, squashes—both summer and winter and such vegetables as Belgian endive, cauliflower, broccoli, and mushrooms.

> 2 tablespoons balsamic vinegar
> 2 tablespoons red wine
> ½ cup olive oil
> 3 garlic cloves, sliced into ovals
> Several sprigs fresh basil, or 1 teaspoon
>   dried basil
> Plenty of freshly ground black pepper

Combine all the ingredients, mixing well. Marinate vegetables for 30 minutes at room temperature, or 1 hour in the refrigerator.

Latin Flavors Marinade   1 cup

Add more or less *jalapeño,* depending on how hot you want this marinade.

> ¼ **cup white wine**
> ½ **cup olive oil**
> **1 small tomato, very finely chopped**
> ½ **onion, chopped**
> **1 fresh or canned** *jalapeño* **pepper, sliced**
>   **into rings**
> **Several sprigs fresh cilantro**

Combine all the ingredients, mixing well. Marinate vegetables for 30 minutes at room temperature, or 1 hour in the refrigerator.

Flavor-infused Oils

Olive oil is a great all-around oil for grilling. It won't burn even at the high temperatures of the grill, and it has a delicious fruity flavor that goes well with most food. Peanut, canola, and safflower oils are good choices as well. Nut oils burn very easily and can give food a bitter taste. Use them carefully, on low grills. They are best used on fruit.

To flavor oil, simply add some pungent or spicy element and let it stand for as little as a day for light flavoring or up to many weeks. Garlic cloves are a popular choice—crush them slightly before adding them to the oil. For a quick garlic oil, heat the oil with crushed garlic cloves over very low for 30 minutes. Take care not to burn the garlic, or it will be bitter. Dried or fresh chilies make spicy oils, and herb sprigs give oil a delicate flavor. A large piece of citrus peel gives oil a bright flavor.

Butter Bastes

Bastes made with butter are wonderful for quick-cooking foods and very easy to prepare. Butter burns easily, so short cooking times are a must. Melt unsalted butter over low heat (you can do this on the grill) and to it add fresh herbs, hot sauce, white wine, garlic, onion, spices such as curry or *garam masala,* or any combination of flavors. For basting on fruits, try a butter baste to which a pinch of sugar, honey, or maple syrup and "sweet" spices such as cinnamon, nutmeg, or allspice have been added.

Brush on food, and baste occasionally as it grills.

Basting Sauce

Basting sauces give vegetables a delicious caramelized crust, while they remain tender and moist on the inside. Take care with any basting sauce that contains sugar (such as barbecue sauce, teriyaki sauce, hoisin sauce, or glazes), since the sugar burns more easily. Keep the fire medium-hot to low, keep the cover over the grill, and check frequently to avoid scorching the food.

> ¼ **cup hoisin sauce**
> **1 tablespoon soy sauce**
> **1 teaspoon dark Asian sesame oil**
> **2 tablespoons peanut oil**
> **1 heaping teaspoon minced fresh ginger**
> **1 garlic clove, finely minced**

Combine all ingredients, mixing well. Baste on vegetables as they grill, taking care not to burn.

In addition to these recipes, a number of recipes for marinades, bastes, oils, and sauces can be found in Chapter 3, Hot off the Grill. These are:

> **Aïoli with Basil, page 69**
> **Butter Baste, page 53**
> **Chipotle Sauce, page 65**
> **Cilantro Sauce, page 50**
> **Coconut, Lime, and Ginger Marinade, page 44**
> **Creamy Lemon Vinaigrette, page 62**
> **Curry-Ginger Sauce, page 69**
> **Fresh Herb Sauce, page 57**
> **Lemon-Mustard Vinaigrette, page 70**
> **Mango Salsa, page 65**
> **Mustard Greens Sauce, page 58**
> **Northern Indian Almond-Spice Sauce, page 74**
> **Orange Cream Sauce, page 73**
> **Parsley-Mint Sauce, page 54**
> **Piquant Green Sauce, page 76**
> **Poppyseed-Orange Vinaigrette, page 69**
> **Red Wine Marinade, page 81**
> **Salsa Cruda, page 79**
> **Satay Sauce, page 85**
> **Sour Cream Sauce, page 83**
> **Soy, Ginger, and Orange Marinade, page 61**
> **Spicy Pecan Nut Butter, page 53**
> **Sweet Lemon Mayonnaise, page 81**
> **Tahini Dressing, page 66**
> **Tangy Dipping Sauce, page 85**

CHAPTER II

A GLOSSARY OF VEGETARIAN FOODS
FOR THE GRILL

Vegetables are easy and rewarding to cook on the grill. A number of vegetables you wouldn't think of grilling are quite delicious cooked by that method. The intense dry heat of the coals sears in flavor and moisture, leaving the best of the flavor intact. Fruit is also a treat when warmed and lightly caramelized on the grill. A variety of other foods, such as breads, tofu and tempeh, and polenta, make wonderful smoky backdrops to grilled vegetables.

This glossary is meant to be a guideline for cooking various vegetables, fruits, and tofu and tempeh on the grill. Each entry consists of a description of flavor and grilling results, tips for shopping, and directions for a basic grilling method. To go beyond the basic method by using a marinade, baste, oil, or sauce, see pages 18–21 for recipes and suggestions.

Most vegetables grill best when brushed lightly with oil beforehand. This keeps them from sticking to the grill and helps the outside sear and crisp. Covering the grill is recommended for the best results, since the cover holds in the intense heat and promotes thorough cooking. A grill basket is an excellent tool for cooking vegetables because smaller chunks won't fall through the rungs of the grill rack, and lots of vegetables can be easily cooked at one time.

Apple
Season: September through January, some varieties year-round.
Varieties: Cortland, Granny Smith, Gravenstein, Rhode Island, Greening, McIntosh, Pippin.
The best apples for the grill are the slightly tart, firm apples listed above. They brown as their sugar begins to caramelize, but retain their shape and crispness. Grilled apples are a delicious, sweet counterpoint to a rich grilled dish, but they are also great served with ice cream for dessert. Look for firm, unbruised fruit.
Basic Grilling Method: Wash apples just before using, core, and cut into wedges or crosswise into slices. The skin helps the slices retain their shape on the grill. Brush the slices lightly with melted butter or oil. Grill over low coals for 10 minutes total, or until lightly browned and tender when pierced with a skewer.

Apricot
Season: May through July.
Varieties: Riland, Moorpark, Royal (Blenheim), Tilton, Chinese (Mormon).
Apricots are surprisingly delicate even with a smoky grill flavor. Apricot season is very short, so be sure that the fruit you choose is as fresh as possible. If they are picked underripe, they will never attain their full flavor and may be mushy and dry. Look for ripe, evenly colored fruit.

Basic Grilling Method: Wash the apricot, slice it in half, and remove the pit (sometimes it helps to twist the halves apart). Brush it lightly with melted butter and grill it cut-side down first. Grill over low coals for about 5 minutes a side.

Artichoke

Season: Year-round, but best in late spring.
Varieties: Globe, purple, baby.

The artichoke is actually the bud of a thistle plant. It has a distinctive, subtle flavor that is delicious slightly seared and smoked on the grill. Look for a heavy artichoke with meaty leaves that are tightly closed. Artichokes should be parboiled (or steamed) whole for 20 to 25 minutes before grilling to speed cooking time. Slice the mostly cooked artichoke in half from top to bottom and scrape out the feathery choke. Brush with oil and grill. Halve or quarter them and scrape out the choke before grilling and cook over low heat or in a foil cup. Brush uncooked baby artichokes with oil and skewer or grill whole in a hinged wire grill basket. Artichoke hearts packed in oil may also be grilled and are delicious.

Basic Grilling Method: Grill halves of artichoke before or after parboiling. Brush with oil and cook over medium-hot coals for 20 to 30 minutes. For a method that does not require pre-cooking, place uncooked artichoke halves (the choke should be scraped out) in a cup formed from aluminum foil, sprinkle with oil and water, and place on the grill for 1 hour.

Asparagus

Season: February through June.
Varieties: Green, purple or violet, white, wild.

Searing asparagus over a hot charcoal fire gives it a delicious roasted flavor and crunch, while the inside remains tender and sweet. Look for firm green stalks with tightly closed buds. To store, trim the ends and stand the bundle upright in about an inch of water in the refrigerator.

Basic Grilling Method: Wash asparagus thoroughly. Instead of snapping the ends off the larger stalks, peel the base to within 3 inches of the tip. Brush the stalks with oil and grill, perpendicular to the cooking grid, over medium-hot coals. Pencil-thin asparagus will be done in about 10 minutes, while thicker stalks will need up to 15 minutes. Turn frequently. Test for doneness with a wooden skewer when asparagus is lightly browned.

Banana

Season: Year-round.
Varieties: Cavendish (yellow), red, dwarf or finger, lemon, plantain.

Bananas are delicious and sweet grilled. The most familiar banana variety is the yellow (Cavendish) banana, but other varieties are gaining in popularity, such as the red banana and the dwarf or finger banana, which have a more intense flavor. Small lemon bananas have a citrus flavor, and large plantains are more savory. Look for slightly underripe bananas, as these will be firmer and less likely to break apart on the grill.

Basic Grilling Method: Peel and slice bananas lengthwise, and brush lightly with melted butter mixed with brown sugar. Grill over medium-hot coals until brown and caramelized but not falling apart, about 10 minutes. When grilled whole in their skins over a low fire, bananas turn custardlike. Cook until the skin is blackened (though not charred) all over, about 12 minutes.

Beet

Season: Year-round.
Varieties: Garden, baby, golden, Chioggia (candy-cane), tubular.

Beets have a rich, assertive flavor that is complemented by the grill. There are many delicious varieties of beets that work well on the grill. In addition to traditional crimson garden beets, there are baby beets, golden (almost orange) beets, Chioggia (red and white striped) beets, and tubular beets. Look for firm, round, medium-sized beets.

Basic Grilling Method: Wash the beets gently, remove the remaining green stems, and cut them into slices. Brush with oil and grill over medium-hot coals for 20 to 25 min-utes, or until tender. Grill baby beets whole for 15 to 20 minutes.

Belgian Endive

Season: Year-round, especially November through April.

The naturally bitter flavor of Belgian endive is complemented by the sweet smoke of the grill, and it is very sim-ple to prepare. Belgian endive has a compact, cigar shape with tightly wrapped leaves. Look for endives about 6 inches long with white leaves that have pale green edges. Discard any withered outside leaves.

Basic Grilling Method: Rinse the endive heads gently under running water and pat dry. Slice in half lengthwise, brush with oil, and place cut-side down on the grill. Cook over medium-hot coals for 7 to 10 minutes, turn, and grill for another 7 to 10 minutes, or until tender and browned.

Bok Choy

(Chinese white cabbage)
Season: Year-round.

This Chinese vegetable looks more like chard than like the old familiar cabbage head we know. Bok choy has deep green leaves and long white stems. On the grill it holds its shape well, and while the edges of the leaves can become crispy, the thick part of the stalk remains crisp on the outside, yet tender and flavorful inside. Look for smaller heads, or quarter larger heads. Baby bok choy and bok choy hearts are also excel-lent grilled.

Basic Grilling Method: Without break-ing off the leaves, wash the head and trim the base. Cut the heads in half lengthwise and brush with oil. Quarter larger heads lengthwise and leave baby bok choy heads whole. Grill cut-side down first on the grill over medium-hot coals for 10 min-utes, turn, and grill for another 10 to 12 minutes, or until tender. Trim the base and serve.

Broccoli

Season: Year-round, especially October through April.

Not only is broccoli one of the most versatile vegetables available, it is also one of the most nutritious—it's a good source of vitamins A and C, as well as calcium and iron. Look for the freshest broccoli bunches with the tightest buds. If they're tightly closed, the main stem will be deep green and the florets will be almost lavender.

Basic Grilling Method: Peel the thick bottom stalks and wash the head thoroughly. Slice into florets with 2-inch stems, and slice the peeled base into chunks. Skewer the chunks. Brush with oil, and cook over medium-hot coals. Florets cook in 10 to 12 minutes, and larger pieces and chunks cook in 18 to 20 min-utes, or until tender when pierced with a skewer.

Brussels Sprouts

Season: September through March.

Brussels sprouts steam and crisp on a covered grill without drying out. They have a delicious, delicate cabbage flavor with a slight nutty taste. Look for the smallest sprouts possible with bright green color and tight heads.

Basic Grilling Method: Since they rarely touch the ground, Brussels sprouts are easy to rinse clean. Trim the bases and remove any yellowed outside leaves. Slice in half length-wise unless very small (these can be skewered whole). Brush the sprouts with oil and arrange in a grill basket or on skewers. Cook over medium-

A Glossary of Vegetarian Foods

tender, 10 to 15 minutes depending on size. Test doneness with a wooden skewer.

Cauliflower

Season: Year-round, especially September through January.
Varieties: White, purple.
Cauliflower adapts itself to almost any kind of marinade, be it spicy, sweet, tangy, or garlicky. Simply oiled and grilled, cauliflower tastes wonderful, too. Grilling enhances the mild flavor of cauliflower, and makes it crunchy and almost nutty. Look for the whitest head with firm and compact florets. The green and purple variety, a hybrid between cauliflower and broccoli, should be prepared more like broccoli (the stems and stalks need to be peeled). It has a mild cauliflower flavor and turns bright green when cooked.
Basic Grilling Method: Wash and trim the head, and break it into large or small chunks. Florets can be skewered or arranged in a hinged wire grill basket. Marinate or brush with oil, and grill over medium-hot coals for 15 to 20 minutes.

Celeriac

(celery root, celery knob, turnip-rooted celery)
Season: October through March.
Celeriac, or celery root, is a knobby, ugly cousin of the celery we usually find. Its texture is similar to that of a potato, but it has a concentrated celery flavor with a hint of sweetness.
Basic Grilling Method: Trim off the stalks and roots. Peel off as much of the brown skin as possible. Slice into ⅓-inch rounds. Brush with oil and grill, like a potato slice, for 7 minutes a side over medium-hot coals, or until tender when pierced with a skewer.

hot coals for 12 to 14 minutes total. Check for doneness with a wooden skewer.

Burdock

(gobo)
Season: Year-round.
This root vegetable is best known and appreciated in Japan, though it grows wild across most of North America. Unfortunately, it may be more known for its above-ground burrs than for the delicious flavor of its underground roots. Burdock's earthy, sweet flavor is reminiscent of artichoke hearts. Its skin is brown and the interior is dull white. Look for roots that are not more than 14 inches long. There is no need to peel burdock.
Basic Grilling Method: Soak the root for 15 minutes or so in salted water to remove bitterness. Rinse well and slice diagonally into ½-inch

ovals, or halve lengthwise and crosswise. Brush with oil and grill over medium-hot coals for about 20 minutes, or until tender.

Carrot

Season: Year-round.
Varieties: Baby, garden, French.
Because grilling carrots crisps and lightly caramelizes the outside, the inside remains sweeter than with almost any other method of cooking. Look for firm smallish to medium carrots (large carrots can be woody) and for a bright, orange color and consistent shape. Those with the green tops attached are the freshest.
Basic Grilling Method: Scrub or peel the carrots. Slice them diagonally into ovals for a grill basket, halve lengthwise, or cook small ones whole. Brush with oil and grill over medium-hot coals until brown and

Corn

Season: *May through September.*
Varieties: *Yellow, white or sweet, blue, baby.*

An undeniable treat during summertime is fresh-roasted corn, and the fresher the corn the better. The moment corn is picked its sugar begins to turn to starch, and its sweet flavor diminishes. If you have corn growing in your garden, start up the coals before you pick it! In the market look for corn with tightly wrapped, deep green husks and dry silk.

Basic Grilling Method: There are two ways to prepare corn for roasting. Using untrimmed corn, pull the husks all the way back leaving them connected to the stalk, forming a sort of husk skirt for the ear, and remove the silk. Baste with butter and grill. Or pull the husks back gently, remove the silk, and pull one or two layers of husk back over the cob. Soak for 10 minutes in water and grill. Corn cooked over medium-hot coals and turned frequently will take 15 to 20 minutes.

Daikon Radish

(Japanese radish, lo bok)
Season: *Year-round.*
Varieties: *White, rose, and black.*

Most supermarkets sell only the long, white, carrot-shaped daikon radishes. Asian markets may also sell the shorter rose and black daikons, both of which are carrot shaped but more irregular and bumpy. Look for firm, almost shiny radishes. Although the Japanese have many different uses for this radish, it's just beginning to catch on here. Daikons roast well on the grill, and the sharp, peppery flavor becomes a bit more muted.

Basic Grilling Method: Wash daikons and peel if desired. Slice daikons diagonally into ovals or into chunks.

Brush with oil and grill over medium-hot coals for 15 to 20 minutes (chunks require more time), or until tender.

Eggplant

(aubergine)
Season: *Year-round, especially August through September.*
Varieties: *Western, Japanese (oriental), Italian (baby), white, Chinese.*

There is a deep, mellow smoky flavor in every bite of grilled eggplant—it is at its best on the grill. The large, pear-shaped Western eggplant is the most common variety, easily recognized by its purple-black skin. Japanese eggplants are long and slender and deep purple. Italian eggplants are pear-shaped like the Western, but smaller and have thinner skins. White eggplants are stark white and completely round or egg-shaped. Their skin tends to be tough, but the interior is more dense and sweet. Small Chinese eggplants, with pale lavender, almost blue skin, are the sweetest, most tender type. All varieties should be firm to the touch and have a fresh, green cap.

There is a debate about whether eggplants need to be salted and drained before they're cooked. This procedure removes moisture and bitterness, but some argue that *fresh* eggplants aren't bitter. In general, larger eggplants, particularly the Western variety, seem to benefit from salting; the smaller ones don't need it. To prepare, slice unpeeled eggplants into rounds, arrange on paper towels, sprinkle with salt, and allow to drain for 30 minutes. Wipe the salt and moisture off and grill.

Basic Grilling Method: Brush eggplant halves, slices, chunks, or small whole eggplants with oil and grill

over medium-hot coals for 10 to 15 minutes a side, or until quite tender and brown.

Fennel

(sweet anise)
Season: *October through March.*
Varieties: *Florence (finocchio).*

When fennel is grilled, its distinctive flavor mellows and deepens with delicious results. Look for a white, softball-sized bulb with celerylike stalks growing up from it. This is the Florence variety—common fennel, which is bulbless, provides the fennel seeds on your spice rack. Avoid yellowed or bruised bulbs with limp, straggly fronds.

Basic Grilling Method: Cut the stalks off even with the top of the bulb, trim the base, and remove the any tough outer layers. Slice the bulb vertically into quarters or ½-inch slices. Brush with oil and grill over medium-hot coals for 20 to 25 minutes, or until tender.

Fig

Season: *June through October.*
Varieties: *Adriatic, Calimyrna, Celeste, Kadota, Magnolia, Mission.*

Even if the thought of doing anything with a fresh fig other than popping it in your mouth seems absurd, one bite of a grilled fig will change that perception. The sweet skin becomes candylike, while the inside is creamy and delicious. Figs are a wonderful accompaniment to any savory dish and are great served with ice cream.

Basic Grilling Method: Rinse figs gently and pat dry. Brush very lightly with oil and place directly on the grill. Cook over medium-hot to low coals for 20 minutes, or until browning.

Garlic

Season: Year-round, especially November through December.
Varieties: Western (white), Mexican or Italian (pink), elephant

Grill-roasted garlic is an exquisite and addictive treat. It becomes mild and sweet and so soft that it can be squeezed right from the papery clove onto slices of toasted bread or grilled vegetables. Elephant garlic, which is milder than the white or pink varieties, can be cooked in the same way. Buy garlic heads that are firm and compact.

Basic Grilling Method: Remove most of the papery layers, leaving all the cloves connected at the base. Place the whole head in a small cup fashioned from heavy-duty aluminum foil. Drizzle about one tablespoon of olive oil over the head of garlic. Fresh herbs such as rosemary or thyme can be tucked in between the cloves. Place the foil cup to the side of a covered grill, and cook garlic heads for 45 minutes to 1 hour, or until the cloves are tender.

Green Onion

(scallion, spring onion)
Season: Year-round, especially May through August.

Green onions are easy to grill and make a nice addition to most grilled dishes. Green onions should have firm white bulbs and fresh-looking green leaves.

Basic Grilling Method: Trim the base and peel off any outside layers that are withered or limp. Trim off all but 3 inches of the green leaves. Brush with oil, and arrange them perpendicular to the grill rungs (so they won't slip through). Grill over medium-hot coals for 10 to 12 minutes, turning frequently for even cooking.

Jerusalem Artichoke

(sunchoke, sunroot)
Season: October through March.

Neither from Jerusalem nor an artichoke, Jerusalem artichokes are native to North America, which makes their name a mystery. Some say the name is an adulteration of *girasole,* their botanical name in Italian. *Girasole* somehow became "Jerusalem," and they do taste something like artichokes. In fact, they are the roots of a hearty variety of sunflower and are now being marketed as sunchokes and sunroots. Jerusalem artichokes are a knobby tuber with a white, crunchy interior. To make both cleaning and cooking simpler, look for smooth, golden-brown skin with as few knobs as possible.

Basic Grilling Method: Clean the root carefully of dirt and grit. Peel if desired but it is not necessary. Small chokes can be brushed with oil and roasted whole. Slice larger chokes into slices or chunks as you would a potato. Brush with oil and cook over medium-hot coals for 10 to 20 minutes, depending on size. Test for doneness with a wooden skewer.

Jícama

(yam bean, Mexican potato)
Season: Year-round, especially November through May.

This brown, turniplike root is crunchy and mildly sweet, and it is unusual but decidedly delicious when grilled. *Jícama* in the market ranges from tennis ball to football sized. Look for unblemished thin skin rather than regularity of shape.

Basic Grilling Method: Slice *jícama* into a manageable size for peeling. Peel off the tough outer skin as well as any fibrous inner skin. Slice into chunks or rounds. Marinate if desired. Cook over medium-hot coals for a total of 20 minutes, or until tender.

Kohlrabi

(cabbage turnip)
Season: April through December.
Varieties: White, purple.
This odd-looking bulb has an elusive, crisp flavor suggesting an amalgam of broccoli, sweet turnips, and radishes. Look for fresh stems (the greens have a delicious peppery taste on their own) on a firm, unbruised, pale green bulb. Choose smaller kohlrabi for more flavor.
Basic Grilling Method: Wash kohlrabi well and carefully pare off the tough peel. Slice into rounds or chunks and brush with oil. Cook over medium-hot coals for 15 to 20 minutes, or until tender when pierced with a skewer.

Leek

Season: Year-round, especially September through November.
The leek is the noble cousin of the garlic and the onion. Though it looks like an overgrown green onion, the leek's flavor is sweeter and more subdued. Look for firm leeks with long, healthy looking green leaves. Choose thinner leeks since the larger ones may be woody. Baby leeks are also delicious grilled whole.
Basic Grilling Method: Trim the roots and the leaves, leaving about 2 inches of green above the white base. Slice the leeks in half lengthwise, and rinse them carefully under running water, gently prying apart the layers to rinse out any sand or grit. Drain them for a few minutes. Brush with oil and grill, cut-side down, over medium-hot coals, for 7 to 10 minutes. Turn and grill for another 7 minutes, or until tender.

Melon

Season: Year-round, especially late summer through early fall.
Varieties: Cantaloupe, Persian melon, Santa Claus (Christmas), Casaba, Crenshaw, Honey Dew.
Although mostly eaten fresh, a slice of melon brushed with a sweet glaze and lightly heated on the grill can be a delightful and unusual treat. Choose ripe varieties, since the melon will only heat and not cook on the grill.
Basic Grilling Method: Halve and seed melons, peel and slice or cut into chunks for skewers. Brush with butter or a sweet glaze and grill over low coals until lightly caramelized, about 5 minutes a side.

Mushroom

Season: Year-round, or depending upon variety.
Varieties: See below.
There is a recent culinary enthusiasm for a wider variety of mushrooms, both cultivated and wild, some of which are described below. In general, look for mushrooms with firm, tight caps; caps that have opened up so the underside is visible show that the mushrooms are past their prime. To store them longer than a day, either place them on a tray in a single layer under a slightly damp paper towel, or in a paper bag. Avoid soaking mushrooms or even washing them under running water as they absorb water readily and will be mushy. Brush them off gently with a damp paper towel, or rinse quickly and pat dry.

Boletus (cèpe, porcino): Available in late spring and fall. These are the richest of the mushrooms, with a silky texture and a flavor that causes celebration when they come into season in parts of Europe. They're cream colored on the inside, dark brown on the outside, with a bulbous stem. The best ones are usually about 6 inches in diameter. Use only fresh (not dried) *boletus* on the grill.

Button (cultivated): Available year-round, these white mushrooms are the common supermarket variety. Their mild flavor is enhanced by a baste or marinade.

Crimini (also Cremini, Roman, browntop): Looking like a brown-capped version of button mushrooms, Crimini taste like them too, but have more flavor.

Oyster: Oyster mushrooms are showing up in more and more produce sections these days. These pearly gray mushrooms have small stems and fan-shaped tops. They grill well, with a rich flavor and light texture. For grilling, look for oyster mushrooms at least 3 inches long.

Portobello: Portobellos are the giants of the mushroom family, with caps up to 8 inches across. They're available in springtime and are usually a deep brown color. Slice the very large ones before grilling them.

Shiitake (Black Forest): These flavorful, parasol-shaped mushrooms are ideal on the grill. They taste terrific marinated or simply brushed with oil and grilled. *Shiitakes* have a firm flesh and a more complex flavor than many of the other mushrooms.

Basic Grilling Method: Clean mushrooms. Marinate or brush with butter or oil, and grill over medium-hot coals for 10 to 15 minutes, depending on variety and size. Test for doneness with a wooden skewer.

wide ribs. Its delicate flavor is enhanced by grilling, which gives it a nutty roasted taste. Look for smaller, firmer heads for grilling.
Basic Grilling Method: Slice cabbage heads into quarters. Brush lightly with oil. Cook over medium-hot coals, cut-side down, for 12 minutes, or until browning. Turn and cook for another 12 to 15 minutes, or until the thickest part is tender when pierced with a skewer. Trim off the base to serve.

Okra

Season: May through October.
Okra yields a surprising result on the grill. It is tender and flavorful on the inside, and the outside takes on a nutty, tasty browned crust. It has a pure okra flavor, since it is cooked on its own rather than in a stew or breaded. Okra can be cooked either whole or halved. Look for firm, small pods with bright color. The large ones (over 4 inches) tend to be fibrous and not very good cooked on the grill.
Basic Grilling Method: Rinse okra and pat dry. Trim off the stem and slice in half if desired. Brush with oil and grill over medium-hot coals until browned and tender, 10 to 20 minutes, depending on size.

Onion

Season: Year-round, depending on variety.
Varieties: Bermuda, Spanish, Italian (also red, purple), yellow (also globe or storage), Maui, Vidalia, Walla Walla, pearl, boiling.
See also *Green Onion*
Grilled onions are a sweet accompaniment to many grilled foods. Combine them with roasted bell peppers and olive oil for a simple relish. Bermuda, Spanish, and Italian or red onions, all fairly mild, taste sweet and smoky when grilled.

Mustard Greens

Season: Year-round, especially December through March.
Mustard greens are far from standard grill fare, but are worth trying. They have a crunchy texture and tangy roasted flavor when grilled. Mustard greens should be deep green with crisp, frilly edges.
Basic Grilling Method: Wash mustard greens thoroughly to remove all sand and dirt. Brush the wet leaves

and stalks lightly with oil, and toss, in a bunch, onto the grill. Turn the bunch frequently with long-handled tongs until they are browning and are wilted and tender, about 10 minutes.

Napa Cabbage

(Chinese cabbage, celery cabbage)
Season: Year-round.
This cabbage looks more like pale green romaine lettuce, with strong

These are best suited to the grill, and are available year-round. White and yellow onions are the most pungent, and should be used with this in mind. Maui, Vidalia, and Walla Walla onions, sweet and juicy enough to be eaten raw, are delicious grilled. These sweet varieties are only available during the summer months. Look for firm onions with no signs of mold or soft spots.

Basic Grilling Method: Peel the papery skin from the onion and trim the top and bottom. Slice into rounds or quarters and brush with oil. Grill rounds flat and quarters skewered or in a hinged wire grill basket. Cook over medium-hot coals for 12 to 18 minutes, depending on size.

Papaya
(pawpaw, tree melon)
Season: Year-round, especially spring and fall.
Varieties: Solo, Sunrise.
Papaya, skewered together with pineapple, brushed with a slightly sweet marinade, and grilled makes an unusual and delightful dessert, particularly with ice cream. Most papayas available in supermarkets weigh about 1½ pounds. The peel can be green, pale yellow, or rosy orange, all with orange flesh. For the best grilling, choose a firm papaya that is not quite ripe.
Basic Grilling Method: Peel the papaya, halve, and remove the seeds (which can be eaten raw). Grill the halves or cut them into cubes or slices. Brush lightly with melted butter and grill over low coals for 15 minutes total, or until browning.

Parsnip
Season: Year-round, especially October through March.
This underappreciated root vege-

table comes to life on the grill. Brushing parsnips with a good olive oil and cooking them over the dry-hot coals seals in the delicious flavor and crunchy texture that is all too often boiled away. Parsnips look like white carrots. Small ones can be cooked whole, and medium-sized parsnips can be sliced lengthwise into ⅓-inch slices. Look for firm, fairly straight parsnips, which are easier to slice.
Basic Grilling Method: Scrub the parsnips but do not peel them. Trim the ends and slice larger ones lengthwise. Parsnips can also be sliced into chunks and skewered or left whole if small. Brush with oil. Grill over medium-hot coals for 12 to 18 minutes, depending on size. Test doneness with a wooden skewer.

Peach
Season: June through October.
Grilled peaches are a sweet accompaniment to a savory dish or a fine dessert served with softly whipped brandied cream or ice cream. Freestone peaches are best for grilling since they can be halved easily and the stone falls free. Look for firm but not rock-hard, unbruised fruit.
Basic Grilling Method: Peel peaches and slice them in half lengthwise. Brush lightly with melted butter and cook over low coals until lightly browning, about 10 minutes total.

Pear
Season: August through December
Varieties: Bartlett, Bosc, Anjou, Comice, Winter Nelis, Seckel
Pears are an easy sweet treat to cook on the grill. They are simply warmed through and slightly caramelized and may be served alongside a savory meal or with ice cream for dessert. Choose firmer pears for the grill but not rock hard ones.

Basic Grilling Method: Halve pears and seed them (there is no need to peel them). Brush lightly with melted butter and cook over low coals until lightly browning, about 10 minutes total.

Pepper, Chili
Season: Year-round.
Varieties: See below.
Fresh chili peppers range in flavor from mildly spicy to firecracker hot. When handling hot chilies, wear rubber gloves and avoid touching your eyes. The hottest parts of the chili are the ribs and seeds—these can be scraped out to cool it down if desired. Look for firm, shiny chilies with no bad spots. Use fresh, not dried chilies, for the grill. Large fresh chilies can be roasted whole and peeled, or stuffed and roasted over a low fire. Small hot chilies, such as Fresnos, *jalapeños, serranos,* and *habaneros* are best used raw in small amounts in marinades or oils rather than roasted.

Anaheim (long green): These mild to hot green chilies are about 7 inches long. When dried ripe Anaheims turn a deep red. Strings (called *ristras*) or wreaths of these dried peppers suggest the delicious food of New Mexico with their characteristic earthy dried red pepper sauces.

Banana (Hungarian Wax): This large mild chili ranges in color from yellow to orange. The Hungarian Wax variety can have a bite; the banana variety is always quite sweet.

Pasillas (chilaca) are popular for their rich, hot flavor. They are usually about 8 inches long and turn deep brown as they ripen. The dried *pasilla* is almost black.

Poblano (the dried form is the *ancho*): The *poblano* is usually 6 inches long and shaped like a slightly flattened green bell pepper. It tastes quite rich, especially when grilled. As it dries, it turns a dark blackish maroon.

Basic Grilling Method: Blacken chili peppers over medium-hot coals. This must be done quickly and carefully to avoid charring the flesh. Place blackened chilies in a paper bag, close it, and let them steam for 15 minutes. Scrape off the black char carefully with the blunt edge of a knife. Remove ribs and seeds if desired. Chilies can be stuffed and grilled over a low fire until tender, about 30 minutes.

Pepper, Sweet Bell
Season: Year-round, especially July through September.
Varieties: Green, red, yellow, purple.

Have peppers on hand for grilling, stuffing, or roasting to add bright color and smoky sweetness to the plate. Their color depends on harvest time: green peppers are picked first. As the pepper continues to ripen on the vine, it turns yellow and then red. Red peppers are the most expensive since they are vine-ripened and therefore sweeter. Purple bell peppers, a different strain from the green, red, and yellow bell, turn greenish gray when cooked. Look for peppers that are firm and smooth-sided, have thick walls, and are heavy for their size.

Basic Grilling Method: Wash the peppers and cut them into halves, quarters, or chunks for skewering. Grill over medium-hot coals until browning and tender, about 10 minutes. To roast, blacken the pepper over red-hot coals until charred all over. Place in a paper bag and allow to steam for 15 minutes. Scrape off the black char with the blunt edge of a knife, seed, and slice. Stuffed peppers will take an hour to cook over medium-hot to low coals.

Pineapple
Season: Year-round, especially March through July.
Varieties: Red Spanish, Cayenne, Sugar Loaf.

The pineapple becomes a delicious treat on the grill. Whether skewered in chunks between other fruits and vegetables, or simply sliced and grilled, it adds a refreshing sweetness and juiciness to the meal. Pineapples (named for their resemblance to pinecones) should have green, rigid leaves and be firm and solid.

Basic Grilling Method: Cut off the green crown and the bottom. Slice downwards around the outside until the skin has been removed. Remove any remaining eyes, and then cut into slices or chunks. Grill over low coals until lightly browned, about 15 minutes total.

Plantain
See *Banana*.

Potato
Season: Year-round.
Varieties: Red, white, long white (White Rose), russet (Idaho), new, Yukon Gold, rose, yellowfin (Finnish yellow wax).
Potatoes are delicious grilled will cook quickly if sliced into rounds or cut into chunks and skewered on metal skewers (the metal conducts heat and cooks the potatoes on the inside). The best potatoes for the grill are white, red, Yukon Golds, new potatoes, and yellowfins. These all have a dense texture and buttery flavor and don't dry out as easily as the russets. Look for firm potatoes without blemishes, sprouts, or green spots. They will keep well in a cool, dark place for over two weeks. Refrigerating potatoes alters their starch and diminishes the flavor.
Basic Grilling Method: Wash the potatoes thoroughly but do not peel. Slice into rounds or ovals, quarter, halve, or cube them. Brush with oil and grill over medium-hot coals for 15 to 25 minutes, depending on size. Potatoes should be tender and browned.

Radicchio
Season: Year-round, especially mid-winter to early spring.
Varieties: Verona, Treviso.
Radicchio is a beautiful burgundy-flecked Italian chicory that grows in small, somewhat loose heads. The leaves are crunchy but tender, with a slightly bitter, peppery flavor. While delicious in salads, radicchio is won-

derfully tasty brushed with olive oil and cooked on the grill.
Basic Grilling Method: Trim the base of the radicchio head without removing it completely, leaving the leaves attached. Slice the entire head in half lengthwise, or into quarters lengthwise if the head is large. Rinse gently under running water and allow to drain. Brush with olive oil and grill over medium-hot coals for 3 to 5 minutes a side, or until browning, and until the thickest part near the base is tender when pierced with a skewer.

Rutabaga
(Swedish turnip)
Season: Year-round, especially August through April.
Like other root vegetables, rutabagas are brought to life on the grill. The dry heat preserves the best aspect of their flavor and texture: a nutty, almost buttery taste and fluffy light flesh. Rutabagas are generally coconut-sized, with thick, brown skin and yellow flesh. Look for small, firm ones, which will be sweeter.
Basic Grilling Method: Wash rutabagas well and peel if large or waxed. Slice into 1/3-inch rounds or chunks. Grill over medium-hot coals for 15 to 18 minutes, or until tender and browned.

Shallot
Season: Year-round, especially springtime.
Shallots grow like garlic, in heads with distinct cloves. But they have a milder, more refined onion flavor that is delicious and sweet when they are roasted on the grill. For grilling, look for shallot heads with the cloves attached.
Basic Grilling Method: Shallots can

be separated into cloves, peeled, brushed with oil and skewered, or the whole heads can be slowly roasted in a foil cup with olive oil until quite tender (see under Garlic for a description). Grill cloves for 15 minutes; whole heads should be roasted on a cooler part of the grill for about 45 minutes.

Snow Pea
See *Sugar Pea*.

Squash, Summer
Season: Year-round, especially May through September.
Varieties: See below.
Nothing could be easier than grilling summer squashes—they are the staples of summer cookouts. Squashes are delicious marinated in any combination of flavors, or they can be simply sliced, oiled, and grilled. There is no need to peel most summer squashes since the skin crisps and holds in moisture. Look for smooth, firm squashes with bright color. Smaller squashes tend to be more flavorful, and the baby varieties are delicious grilled whole.

Chayote (vegetable pear, mirliton): This native American squash has only recently come to be appreciated. It has firm, very dense flesh with superb flavor. *Chayote* are typically pear shaped, pale green, and ridged. The skin should be peeled, a task most easily performed under running water since it has a slippery feel.

Crookneck (yellow): This pale to bright yellow squash has a bulbous end and a long thin neck that curves at the top. It's a typical summer squash, with thin skin (buy it if your fingernail pierces it easily), soft

seeds, and a mild flavor. Look for squashes no longer than 6 inches or for baby squash.

Pattypan (scallop squash, scaloppini): This squash is circular and flat with scalloped edges. It can be almost white, yellow, or pale green. The most recent pattypan variety, scaloppini, is a cross with zucchini and is dark green.

Zucchini (courgette): The most popular summer squash, the deep green cylindrical zucchini is a star on the grill. The most flavorful are the smaller ones and baby zucchini is delicious.

Basic Grilling Method: Wash and trim the squash but do not peel (except *chayote*). Cut it into chunks, halve lengthwise, or grill whole, brushed with oil, over medium-hot coals. Most squashes cook in under 15 minutes total. Test doneness with a skewer.

Squash, Winter
Season: Year-round, especially September through March.
Varieties: See below.

The grilling season need not end on Labor Day, since in most parts of the country the weather is gorgeous on through October. Then grilling is a treat—an aromatic charcoal fire on a crisp evening can be the perfect backdrop for a memorable dinner. This is the winter squash season in America, the land where squashes abound. They are wonderful when charcoal-roasted with dry heat and flavored with grill smoke.

Acorn (table queen): This acorn-shaped, ribbed squash is typically about 6 inches long and a deep, dark green with occasional orange spots (though a bright orange variety is

sometimes available). It stays moist when roasted. Grill it with the skin to hold its shape. Acorn squash is best halved, seeded, and grilled for 40 to 60 minutes.

Banana: Large banana squash can grow up to 2 feet long, but look for smaller ones for the grill. Their skin is banana yellow, and they have orange flesh. Peel and grill chunks on skewers or in a hinged grill basket.

Buttercup: This little dark green squash looks as if it is wearing a small blue beret. The buttercup, a variety of turban squash, is very smooth and sweet. The buttercup is quick-cooking and sweeter when steamed (chunks) for 5 minutes before grilling, but delicious and savory when slow cooked.

Butternut: The large pear-shaped butternut squash is great on the grill. The pale brown skin is remarkably thin for a winter squash, so it can be grilled with or without it. This squash is easily cut into rounds for grilling and has a nutty, sweet taste. To roast, slice in half, seed, and cook for 40 to 60 minutes.

Delicata (sweet potato squash): As the name suggests, this squash has a delicate flavor. It is shaped like a fat cucumber. Delicatas have an edible skin that is cream-colored with green striations. Steam slices or chunks until barely tender and then grill, or grill uncooked chunks or halves.

Hubbard: This squash looks like a large, bumpy crookneck squash. The thick skin is greenish orange, and the orange flesh tends to be a bit stringy. Peel and steam slices or chunks until barely tender and then grill. Roast raw chunks or halves.

Kabocha: This sweet squash tastes wonderful when grilled. It is bumpy and deep green with lighter green streaks. It can also be orange. Buy the 2- to 3-pound size. *Kabochas* should be peeled before grilling. It is tough to cut and peel, but well worth the effort.

Basic Grilling Method: Peel the squash if necessary and remove the seeds. Cut into slices or chunks. You can steam them until barely tender before grilling (if you are in a hurry and don't want to slow-roast the squash, this is a shortcut). Brush with oil and grill over medium-hot coals. Uncooked slices and chunks require 20 to 25 minutes to cook. To roast halved squash, seed the halves and brush with oil. Cook cut-side down for 20 minutes, turn and cook 20 to 30 minutes more, or until tender. Test doneness with a wooden skewer.

Sugar Pea
Season: Year-round.
Varieties: Snow pea (mangetout, Chinese pea), sugar snap pea.

The two familiar sugar peas we know are the plump sugar snap pea and the flat snow pea. Both fall into the category of edible-pod pea—sweet, crunchy peas that are eaten pod and all. They cook quickly on the grill and best in a hinged wire grill basket along with other vegetables. Look for small, bright green pods. Avoid yellowed or limp pods and, if you taste one in the store, you can avoid stringy ones as well.

Basic Grilling Method: Wash peas and string them if needed. The snow pea will have a string along one side only; the sugar snap pea may have a tough string along both seams.

A Glossary of Vegetarian Foods

waffelike cake that absorbs marinades with gusto and can take on any flavor you combine it with. Look for fresh tempeh in the refrigerated section of health food stores. The varieties that include other ingredients, such as brown rice or quinoa, are more flavorful than the plain tempeh. Marinate (it needs it) for an hour before grilling. Store tempeh for no more than a week refrigerated.

Basic Grilling Method: Grill marinated tempeh whole, or cut into strips or chunks, over medium-hot coals for 15 minutes, or until well browned.

Tofu
(bean curd)
Varieties: Firm, extra-firm.

Like tempeh, tofu is made from soybeans, and is high in protein and low in cholesterol. Tofu is a sort of smooth cheese made from soy milk, which is pressed into blocks. It is so mild and spongy that it takes on whatever flavors it is marinated in, which is nice for grilling. Only use firm or extra-firm tofu for grilling; other varieties (soft and silken) will fall apart on the grill. Use tofu within a week. It keeps best when refrigerated, covered with water that is changed daily.

Basic Grilling Method: Before grilling tofu, drain off the liquid and place the tofu cake between several layers of paper towels. Place a plate on top and let stand for 1 to 3 hours, changing the paper towels occasionally. Marinate it whole or in slices or cubes for at least 30 minutes. Skewer carefully, using 2 parallel skewers to secure larger slices. Oil the grill to prevent sticking. Grill over medium-hot coals for 10 to 15 minutes, or until well browned.

Brush the pea pods with oil, arrange in a grill basket, and grill over medium-hot coals for 5 minutes total.

Sweet Potato
Season: Year-round, especially September through April.
Varieties: Boniato (Cuban sweet potato, white sweet potato), yam (a misnomer).

Sweet potatoes have an identity problem. They are not potatoes (they are, however, sweet) and are also distinct from the true yam (see Yam). The common supermarket varieties are the yellow-skinned, pale orange-fleshed potato and the more moist, dark orange variety that is often mislabeled as a yam. Both varieties, however, are quite delicious when grilled. The boniato, a more unusual sweet potato, has amost white flesh and a delicate,

sweet flavor. Look for smooth, unbroken skin and firm ends. Do not refrigerate sweet potatoes.

Basic Grilling Method: Scrub sweet potatoes, trim the ends, and slice lengthwise into ovals, crosswise into rounds, or into chunks for skewering on metal skewers. Brush with oil and grill over medium-hot coals for 15 to 20 minutes, or until tender when pierced with a skewer.

Tempeh
Varieties: Added flavors such as brown rice, quinoa, mixed grains.

Though tempeh hasn't caught on as quickly as some had hoped, it may yet, given that it is very high in protein and very low in cholesterol. It is also a great grill food. Tempeh is made from split soybeans that are cultured with a starter and allowed to "ferment." The result is a firm

Tomatillo

(Mexican green tomato, tomate verde)
Season: Year-round, especially June through September.

The little *tomatillo* looks like hard, green tomato covered with a papery husk. It has a tart flavor that mellows when grilled. Since *tomatillos* are firm, they hold their shape well on the grill. *Tomatillos* are naturally hard, so soft ones are spoiled. Look for evenly green fruit that has the papery husk attached.

Basic Grilling Method: Clean the *tomatillos,* removing the husk if desired, and stem. Grill whole (be sure to prick the skin to keep it from exploding) or sliced into halves or slices, or cut into chunks. Brush with oil and cook over medium-hot coals until tender and browned, about 15 minutes.

Tomato

Season: Year-round, especially June through September.
Varieties: Beefsteak, globe, plum (Italian or Roma), cherry, green, yellow pear.

A grilled tomato makes a great relish for any grilled sandwich, and adds a smoky, citrusy flavor to any dish it accompanies. Winter tomatoes tend to be pink and flavorless; in springtime choose cherry or plum tomatoes, which will have more flavor. The rich, fruity flavor of a vine-ripened tomato is unparalleled, so be sure to scout them out in summer. Tomatoes for grilling should be firmer than those you pick for slicing and eating raw. Yellow and green varieties are often firm and, while not as flavorful, add color to the plate. Baby yellow, orange, and red pear and plum tomatoes are delicious grilled whole. Do not refrigerate any variety of tomato.

Basic Grilling Method: Wash tomatoes and cut larger ones into slices, halves, or quarters for skewering, brush with oil, and grill over medium-hot coals. Cherry and baby plum tomatoes can be skewered and grilled whole. Tomatoes cook in 8 to 10 minutes, or until warm and slightly browned. Do not overcook them.

Turnip

Season: Year-round, especially October through February.

Turnips are another root vegetable that have a light, crisp texture and tangy, succulent flavor when grilled. Look for turnips that are no larger than apples, since these will be sweeter. The skin should be firm and smooth, white with pink streaks near the top, and the leaves attached as a indicator of freshness. Tiny baby turnips are quite delicious skewered and grilled.

Basic Grilling Method: Wash and trim turnips. Peel larger turnips. Baby turnips can be skewered and cooked whole; cut larger turnips into slices or chunks. Brush with oil and grill over medium-hot coals until tender when pierced with a skewer, 15 to 20 minutes.

Yam

See also Sweet Potato.
Season: Sporadically available year-round.

Most of the "yams" sold in the supermarket are more likely to be the dark orange variety of the sweet potato. The true yam is not grown commercially in this country but is a staple in South and Central America, West Africa, and in parts of Asia and the South Pacific. The tuberous root of a tropical vine, this strange vegetable can be the size of a small potato or it can grow to over 6 feet long and weigh several hundred pounds. True yams are available in some Latin markets, either whole or more commonly in chunks sold by the pound. They are brown, beige, or almost black, and their flesh tends to be pale yellow or cream colored.

Basic Grilling Method: Wash and peel the yam under running water since it has a slippery feel. Slice it or cut it into chunks. Brush with oil and grill over medium-hot coals for 15 to 20 minutes, or until tender and browned.

Yard-long Bean

(Chinese long bean, asparagus bean)
Season: Year-round, especially September through November.

This interesting bean is part of the black-eyed pea rather than the bean family. It does grow to be a yard long, although the better flavored beans are no longer than 18 inches and pencil thin. The yard-long bean is less firm and crisp than a green bean, so the indicator of freshness will be a plump bean with an even green coloring.

Basic Grilling Method: Wash the beans and pat dry. Marinate or brush with oil and grill over medium-hot coals, turning frequently, for 8 to 10 minutes. Cook them perpendicular to the grill rungs, turning frequently. Yard-long beans can also be twisted into a pretzel shape, oiled or marinated, and grilled.

A Glossary of Vegetarian Foods

CHAPTER III

HOT OFF THE GRILL

Spicy Black Beans and Corn · Grilled Red Onion Slices

Serves 6

Polenta, a dense Italian corn cake made from coarsely ground cornmeal (also called *polenta*), is mixed with spice and bright colored red peppers and served with earthy flavors that are better known in New Mexico than in Italy. A simple salad of sliced avocado and papaya sprinkled with lime juice, salt, and coarsely ground black pepper goes well with this hearty meal.

Polenta with Green Chili and Red Pepper

Fresh green chilies can be mild or intensely hot. The seeds and ribs are the hottest part of the chili, so remove them if you suspect your chili to be a scorcher. Anaheims are often mild, and the banana chili is almost too mild. *Jalapeños* are delicious here if heat is the objective.

> 6½ cups water
> 1½ teaspoons salt
> 1½ cups polenta or coarsely ground cornmeal
> ¼ cup chopped green chilies, fresh or canned
> ½ red pepper, seeded and sliced into matchsticks
> 3 tablespoons butter
> Olive oil

Bring the water to a boil in a large, heavy saucepan. Add the salt. Reduce the heat and add the polenta very slowly, stirring constantly with a wooden spoon to prevent lumps. Cook over low heat, stirring frequently, for 25 to 35 minutes. Halfway through cooking, add the green chilies and red pepper slices. As the polenta thickens, press out any lumps on the side of the pan. The polenta is done when it pulls away from the sides of the pan.

Beat the butter into the cooked polenta and spread it into a buttered 8-inch square or 10-inch round pan or dish. Cool for an hour or more.

Slice the polenta into squares or wedges and brush with olive oil. On an open or closed grill over medium-hot coals, grill the polenta slices until lightly browned and heated through, 8 to 10 minutes per side. Serve with Spicy Black Beans and Corn.

Spicy Black Beans and Corn

If time is short, you may substitute canned black beans, drained of their liquid.

> 2½ cups dried black beans or 6 cups cooked canned beans
> 2 tablespoons olive oil
> 2 large garlic cloves, finely minced
> 1 cup fresh or frozen corn kernels
> 1 cup orange juice (2 to 3 oranges)
> Several dashes hot sauce, or to taste
> ¼ cup chopped cilantro leaves
> ½ teaspoon salt, or to taste
> Chopped cilantro
> Grated cheese
> Sour cream

Wash and pick over the dried beans. Soak overnight in plenty of water, or, for quick soaking, bring them to a rolling boil with plenty of water in a large pot, remove from heat, and let stand covered for 1 hour.

Drain the soaked dried beans. Put them back in the pot and cover with plenty of water. Bring to a boil, then reduce the heat and simmer, uncovered, until the beans are tender but still hold their shape, approximately 45 minutes. Drain.

Meanwhile, heat the oil in a large saucepan and sauté the garlic over medium heat for 2 or 3 minutes. Add the cooked beans, corn, orange juice, hot sauce, cilantro, and salt. Simmer uncovered for 25 minutes or until all the liquid is absorbed and the beans are tender. Serve over the grilled polenta and pass chopped cilantro, grated cheese, and sour cream for toppings.

Grilled Red Onions

> 2 large red onions
> 2 tablespoons olive oil
> Dash of salt

Trim the top and bases of the onions, peel off the papery outside layers, and slice into ⅓-inch slices. Brush with olive oil, sprinkle with salt, and grill over medium-hot coals, turning once, for 10 minutes per side.

Hot off the Grill

COCONUT, LIME, AND GINGER-MARINATED VEGETABLES

Silver Noodles with Basil

Coconut, Lime, and Ginger-marinated Vegetables

Lemongrass is available in Asian markets that carry Thai and Vietnamese produce. If fresh is unavailable, use the dried whole or chopped leaves and skip lining the grill basket. Use any combination of the following vegetables for the dish.

> Coconut, Lime, and Ginger Marinade
> (see below)
> Zucchini, sliced in half lengthwise
> Carrots, sliced in half lengthwise
> Cherry or plum tomatoes
> Fresh *shiitake* mushrooms
> Asparagus, trimmed and bases peeled if fibrous
> Broccoli, separated into large florets
> Green onions
> 2 stalks lemongrass

Prepare the Coconut, Lime, and Ginger Marinade. Prepare the vegetables and set them aside to marinate for 30 minutes. Pull off the tougher, outer leaves of the lemongrass, reserving the tender inner bulb for the marinade. Begin soaking the lemongrass leaves in water.

Loosely arrange half the lemongrass leaves on the bottom of a hinged wire grill basket. Arrange the marinated vegetables on top and place the remaining leaves of grass on the vegetables. Close and secure the basket.

Place the grill basket on the rack of an open grill over medium-hot coals. Grill for 5 to 7 minutes per side, or until the vegetables are browning (where exposed) and tender when pierced with a skewer.

Coconut, Lime, and Ginger Marinade

Nam pla, a fermented fish sauce, is an essential ingredient in Thai cuisine. Its pungency mellows as it cooks. Soy sauce can be used in place of *nam pla,* which will produce a less pungent, slightly sweeter marinade.

> ¾ cup canned coconut milk
> 1 tablespoon grated lime zest
> ½ small dried red chili, seeded and minced
> 2 garlic cloves, minced
> 1 tablespoon shredded fresh ginger
> 1 bulb fresh lemongrass (the pale, tender inner stalks), minced, or 1 tablespoon minced dried lemongrass
> 1 tablespoon *nam pla*
> 2 tablespoons peanut oil
> Juice of ½ lime
> Pinch of brown sugar

Combine all the ingredients in a blender or food processor and process until smooth.

Silver Noodles with Basil

Although basil may seem like an odd ingredient here, it is very commonly used in Thai cooking.

> 1 recipe Coconut, Lime, and Ginger Marinade
> (see above)
> 6 ounces dried rice vermicelli
> 4 sprigs fresh basil

Prepare the marinade, or use what is remaining after marinating the vegetables for the recipe shown above. Chop most of the leaves from the basil sprigs, reserving the tops for garnish. Add the chopped basil to the marinade.

Bring a large pot of water to a boil. Drop the noodles into the boiling water, turn off the heat, and let stand 5 minutes. Drain well in a colander and cool. Toss the noodles with the marinade to coat. Arrange the basil tops on each serving.

Serves 6

Since the weather often stays quite beautiful well into fall, cooking outdoors need not be limited to summer. Nothing stimulates the appetite more than the smell of a charcoal fire on a brisk fall evening. Squash and wild rice are autumn flavors; serve this seasonal dish with a salad of peeled and sliced oranges, fresh fennel, and toasted pecans.

Roasted Acorn Squash

Select acorn squashes that are heavy, firm, and deep green.

> 3 medium-sized acorn squash
> Olive oil

Slice the squashes in half lengthwise and brush both the skins and flesh with oil.

Grill, covered, over medium-hot to low coals cut-side down, then skin-side down, until tender when pierced with a skewer, approximately 40 minutes.

Wild Rice Salad

Wild rice is an unusual grain. It is not a rice at all but the seeds of a swamp-growing grass. It grows wild in Minnesota (where it is *quite* popular) and was for years harvested by hand. It is now cultivated and is more widely available and considerably less expensive.

> 1½ cups wild rice
> 4½ cups vegetable broth or water
> ½ teaspoon salt
> ½ cup hazelnuts
> 2 tablespoons currants
> 4 heaping tablespoons minced fresh chives
> Juice of ½ orange
> Dash of white wine or champagne vinegar
> ¼ teaspoon ground ginger

Rinse the rice well in a colander and allow to drain. In a large saucepan, bring the vegetable broth or water and salt to a boil. Add the rice, reduce the heat, and simmer, covered, for approximately 35 to 40 minutes. The kernels should be slightly firm, not mushy. Drain well and cool.

While the rice is cooking, toast the hazelnuts in a preheated 350° oven for 7 minutes. Rub off the papery skins and chop coarsely.

Toss the cooled rice, chopped hazelnuts, currants, and chives together in a large bowl. Whisk the orange juice, vinegar, and ginger together and sprinkle it over the rice, tossing well to combine.

Vegetables on the Grill

Smoked Gouda and Roasted Peppers on Rosemary Bread · Blue Cheese on Nut Bread
Swiss with Red Onion and Whole-grain Mustard on Rye · Feta and Fennel on Italian Bread

Serves 8

Making these open-faced sandwiches on the grill is an on-going process that becomes a casual and delicious party. Serve them with your favorite composed salads and thick-cut potato chips, with plenty of cold drinks. Have a big tray with every-thing on hand near the grill for cooking and assembling the sandwiches. A somewhat low fire is required for breads with cheese, since you want the cheese to melt before the bread is burned. Spread the coals out and par-tially close the vents to keep the fire low.

Smoked Gouda and Roasted Peppers on Rosemary Bread

Before starting the sandwiches, blacken the peppers on the grill over the flames, peel, and slice (see page 34 for more detailed information). Smoked Gouda can be soft, and may be easier to grate than slice.

> 2 red bell peppers
> 2 yellow bell peppers
> ¼ cup olive oil
> 2 teaspoons balsamic vinegar
> 3 tablespoons chopped fresh parsley
> Salt to taste
> Freshly ground black pepper
> 1 loaf rosemary bread
> ½ pound smoked Gouda
> Olive oil
> 2 peeled garlic cloves

Roast the peppers and peel, slice, and toss them with the olive oil, vinegar, parsley, salt, and black pepper. Slice the bread and the cheese. Have the roasted peppers, bread and cheese (sliced or grated), olive oil, and peeled garlic cloves on hand.

Toast one side of the bread on the grill. Brush the toasted side with olive oil and rub lightly with a garlic clove. Turn and toast the other side. Arrange the cheese on top and place a dab of peppers on top of the cheese. Cook until the cheese is melted and bubbly, taking care not to burn the bread.

Blue Cheese on Nut Bread

Maytag blue cheese is a sweet, young blue from Wisconsin, which is the most delicious choice for this open-faced sandwich. Simply toast nut bread slices and spread the warm bread with blue cheese. Then top it with a few slices of peppery radish or a leaf of a tart green, such as arugula, endive, or watercress.

Swiss with Red Onion and Whole-grain Mustard on Rye

> 1 loaf rye bread
> ½ pound Swiss cheese
> 2 medium-sized red onions
> Whole-grain mustard

Slice the bread, cheese, and red onions. Have all the ingredients on hand. Toast one side of the bread on the grill. Spread mustard on the toasted side, put the cheese on top, and return the bread to the grill, un-toasted side down. Cook until the cheese is melted, taking care not to burn the bread. Place a slice of red onion on top and serve.

Feta and Fennel on Italian Bread

Cook the fennel on the grill before starting the sandwiches. It can be cooked on a cooler side of the grill while you wait for the coals to burn down enough for grilling bread.

> 3 fresh fennel bulbs
> Olive oil
> Salt and freshly ground black pepper, to taste
> 1 loaf Italian bread
> ½ pound feta cheese
> 2 peeled garlic cloves

Trim, halve, and brush the fennel bulbs with olive oil. Grill over medium-hot coals until brown and tender, approximately 20 minutes. Remove and slice into thin strips. Toss with a little olive oil and season to taste with salt and pepper.

Slice the bread. Have the bread, cheese, olive oil, peeled garlic cloves, and roasted fennel on hand. Grill one side of the bread on the grill. Brush the toasted side with olive oil and rub lightly with a garlic clove. Turn and toast the other side. Spread cheese on the toasted bread and top with a few strips of fennel.

Avocado and Jack Cheese Quesadillas

Serves 4

A citrus flavor is often a delicious counterpoint to grilled food. In this recipe that citrus flavor comes from cilantro, which has a distinct pungency not unlike lemons, but a mellow savory flavor that balances the tanginess. This dish is best with plain steamed rice so as not to mask the bright flavors.

Grilled Skewered Vegetables with Cilantro Sauce

Any variety of fresh vegetable can be skewered, grilled, and eaten with this flavorful sauce. Cilantro is a *very* aromatic, lacy-leaved herb, used most commonly in Asian and South and Central American cuisines.

> Cilantro Sauce (see below)
> 3 tablespoons butter
> 1 tablespoon olive oil
> 1 clove garlic, finely minced
> ½ teaspoon ground cumin
> *Chayote* squash, peeled under running water, sliced into ½-inch chunks, and parboiled for 5 minutes
> *Jícama,* peeled and sliced into ½-inch chunks
> Corn on the cob, sliced into 1-inch rounds
> Cherry tomatoes
> Zucchini, sliced into ½-inch chunks
> Pattypan squash, sliced into ½-inch chunks
> Red onion, quartered and separated into 3-layer pieces
> Bell peppers, seeded and sliced into ½-inch chunks

Prepare the Cilantro Sauce and set aside until needed. In a small saucepan heat the butter, oil, garlic, and cumin. Use this as a baste while grilling the vegetables. Grill the vegetables on a closed grill over medium-hot coals, turning to cook all sides, until browned and tender when pierced with a skewer, 15 to 20 minutes for most vegetables. Serve with warm Cilantro Sauce.

Cilantro Sauce

> 1 cup cilantro leaves, tightly packed (about ½ a bunch)
> ½ cup parsley leaves, tightly packed
> 2 green onions, white part and half the green leaves, coarsely chopped
> 1 garlic clove, chopped
> 1 teaspoon lime juice
> Dash of nutmeg
> ¾ cup heavy cream or half-and-half
> Salt and freshly ground black pepper to taste

Combine the cilantro, parsley, green onions, garlic, lime juice, and nutmeg in a food processor and purée. Scrape into a small saucepan and add the cream. Heat gently to thicken, about 10 minutes. Season to taste with salt and pepper.

Avocado and Jack Cheese Quesadillas

Quesadillas are fast and easy on the grill. Serve with hot salsa or Cilantro Sauce.

> 2 avocados
> ½ a lemon
> Salt and pepper to taste
> ½ pound Monterey Jack cheese, thinly sliced
> 16 fresh corn or flour tortillas

Peel, seed, and slice the avocado. Squeeze lemon juice over the avocado slices to keep them from discoloring. Season with salt and pepper if desired.

Arrange the cheese slices on half the corn tortillas and place them over medium-hot coals. When the cheese is melted and bubbly, about 3 minutes, top each with several avocado slices and another corn tortilla, and turn. Cook for 3 minutes on the other side, remove, and slice into quarters. Serve hot.

Vegetables on the Grill

Serves 4

A salad of mixed greens with tangy sorrel in it goes well with the sweet flavors of yams and apples.

Yams, Apples, and Leeks Grilled with Spicy Pecan Nut Butter

> Spicy Pecan Nut Butter (see below)
> Butter Baste (see below)
> 2 medium-sized yams, sliced lengthwise into ⅓-inch-thick slices
> 2 Granny Smith apples, cored and sliced crosswise into ⅓-inch-thick slices
> 2 leeks, trimmed, leaving 1 inch of green leaves, and halved lengthwise

Prepare the Spicy Pecan Nut Butter and set aside.

Prepare the Butter Baste (the recipe makes enough baste for the whole ears of corn in addition to the vegetables). Brush the vegetables with the baste and grill over medium-hot coals on a covered grill for 5 to 7 minutes per side. The apples burn more readily, so keep them to a cooler side of the grill. Serve the vegetables with a dollop of nut butter on the side.

Spicy Pecan Nut Butter

This creamy sauce that has the consistency of peanut butter is delicious alongside the flavorful yams, apples, and leeks.

> 1 cup unsalted pecans, chopped
> ⅓ small yellow onion, coarsely chopped
> 1 tablespoon spicy mustard
> 1 tablespoon orange juice
> ½ teaspoon Tabasco sauce
> 1 tablespoon honey
> 1 tablespoon olive oil
> 4 tablespoons water

Toast the pecans in a preheated 350° oven for 7 minutes, or until they begin browning. Combine all the ingredients in a food processor and process until smooth. The mixture should be thick and light.

Whole Corn on the Cob with Spicy Butter

Leave the husks peeled back but attached at the base to use as a sort of handle for turning the corn on the grill and eating it when it is done. White corn tends to be sweeter and less chewy than its yellow cousin.

> Butter Baste (see below)
> 4 whole, unhusked ears of white corn

Prepare the Butter Baste, or use the remaining Butter Baste from the recipe for Yams, Apples, and Leeks (above). Gently pull the corn husks away from the ears, leaving them connected to the base of the ear and taking care not to snap them off. Remove the silk. Brush the ears liberally with Butter Baste and grill on a open or closed grill over medium-hot coals until browning and tender when pierced with a skewer, 10 to 12 minutes. Brush again with Butter Baste and serve.

Butter Baste

This makes enough baste for all the yams, apples, leeks, and corn.

> 6 tablespoons butter
> 1 large garlic clove, finely minced
> 1 tablespoon white vinegar
> Several dashes of Tabasco sauce
> ¼ teaspoon cayenne pepper
> 1 tablespoon fresh chopped thyme leaves, or ¼ teaspoon dried thyme
> ¼ teaspoon salt, or to taste

In a small saucepan, melt the butter over low heat. Whisk in the garlic, vinegar, Tabasco, cayenne, thyme, and salt.

Hot off the Grill

Serves 6

Fresh figs, although very delicate, are delicious grilled and retain their shape beautifully. Their soft flesh absorbs the flavor of smoke, and they crisp on the outside, remaining tender and succulent inside. Prepare a fire with hot and cool spots for this combination of figs and vegetables.

Fresh Figs and Vegetables

Cèpes, Portobello, or oyster mushrooms, sliced into quarters, can be used in place of the Crimini mushrooms.

> 6 tablespoons butter
> ¼ cup brandy
> 4 shallot heads, or 20 shallot cloves
> 12 French or small carrots
> Parsley-Mint Sauce (see below)
> 12 small zucchini
> 12 fresh figs
> 24 Crimini mushrooms

Melt the butter and add the brandy. Simmer briefly to reduce the brandy. Remove and set aside in a warm place.

Separate the shallots into cloves, peel them, and trim the root ends. Brush them liberally with the brandied butter and place in a loose cup fashioned out of aluminum foil, leaving the top open. Cook on a covered grill away from the hottest coals for 45 minutes, or until tender when pierced with a skewer.

Scrub the carrots and trim off all but 1 inch of the green top. Halve longer carrots. Brush with brandied butter and grill, covered, away from the hottest coals, for 30 minutes.

Meanwhile, prepare the Parsley-Mint Sauce and set aside.

Wash, trim, and halve the zucchini lengthwise. Brush the zucchini and figs with brandied butter. Skewer the mushrooms and brush with brandied butter. Grill zucchini, figs, and mushrooms over medium-hot coals for 15 to 20 minutes, turning occasionally for even browning. Serve with Parsley-Mint Sauce.

Parsley-Mint Sauce

A fresh-tasting dipping sauce for grilled vegetables.

> 1 cup firmly packed parsley leaves
> ⅓ cup mint leaves
> 1 cup nonfat plain yogurt
> ½ teaspoon ground fenugreek (optional)
> 1 tablespoon olive oil
> Pinch of sugar

Combine all the ingredients in a blender or food processor and process until smooth.

Couscous

Couscous is the staple grain of North African cuisine. It is a granular form of semolina, made from durum wheat. Use the precooked or quick-cooking variety of couscous, which can be found in Middle Eastern markets and most large supermarkets. The whole wheat varieties have a more robust flavor.

> 2½ cups vegetable broth or water
> 1 tablespoon olive oil
> Pinch of salt
> 1½ cups quick-cooking couscous
> Pinch of saffron

Bring the broth or water, oil, and salt to a boil in a large saucepan. Stir in the couscous, cover, and remove the pan from the heat. Let stand 7 minutes. Sprinkle saffron over the top of the couscous and fluff with a fork to combine. Use enough saffron to give the couscous a yellow tint.

Vegetables on the Grill

Serves 4

Despite their high price, baby vegetables are worth seeking out. They have a delicate, sweet flavor that is seared in on the grill and are a convenient size for skewering whole. Most varieties cook in the same amount of time. Select any combination of these tiny vegetables, looking for the freshest and firmest ones.

Baby Vegetables with Pasta and Fresh Herb Sauce

If baby vegetables are unavailable, cut up larger vegetables and cook them separately on skewers. Mushrooms, though not a "baby" vegetable, cook in the same amount of time and are delicious with pasta. Try using pasta shells in this recipe for variety.

> ¼ cup olive oil
> 1 dried red chili
> 2 garlic cloves, slightly crushed
> Fresh Herb Sauce (see below)
> 2 pounds assorted baby vegetables, such as zucchini, summer squash, pattypan squash, tiny beets, eggplant, pear tomatoes, artichokes
> 1 pound dried pasta
> 1 tablespoon salt
> Parmesan cheese

Heat the oil over low in a small saucepan with the red chili and crushed garlic cloves for 10 minutes to release the chili and garlic oils. Set aside. Prepare the Fresh Herb Sauce and set aside.

Skewer all the vegetables and brush with the flavored oil. On an open or covered grill, cook the vegetable skewers, turning occasionally, for 15 to 20 minutes, or until they begin browning and are tender when pierced with a skewer.

Meanwhile, cook the pasta in 4 quarts of boiling salted water until *al dente*. Drain and immediately toss with the sauce. Serve with the grilled vegetables. Sprinkle Parmesan cheese on top.

Fresh Herb Sauce

A delicious and light sauce for pasta.

> ⅓ cup extra virgin olive oil
> 1 tablespoon lemon juice
> Zest of ¼ lemon
> 1 heaping tablespoon chopped fresh chives
> 1 heaping tablespoon chopped fresh Italian parsley
> 2 heaping tablespoons chopped fresh basil
> 1 tablespoon fresh thyme leaves
> Salt to taste
> Plenty of freshly ground black pepper
> Grated Parmesan to taste

Heat the olive oil gently in a small saucepan. Do not let it smoke. Just when the pasta is ready, remove the oil from the heat. To the oil add the lemon juice, lemon zest, chives, parsley, basil, thyme, salt and pepper and immediately toss with hot pasta. Serve with grated Parmesan.

Hot off the Grill

The tangy sauce made from mustard greens is the perfect accompaniment to grilled root vegetables. Kasha, or toasted buckwheat, has a mild nutty flavor that makes a nice backdrop for this dish. Add minced chives or green onions to kasha for color and a little bite.

Root Vegetables

Metal skewers are a must for root vegetables. Because the metal heats through and cooks the inside of the vegetables while the outside is seared by the coals, cooking times are shortened. The vegetables listed below are suggestions—select what is fresh and in season, and what you like. The glossary gives more specific information for each vegetable.

> Potatoes of different varieties
> Sweet potatoes
> Yams
> Turnips
> Parsnips
> Carrots
> Torpedo onions
> Small or baby beets
> Leeks
> Jerusalem artichokes
> Olive oil
> Salt

Peel those vegetables that have tough or fibrous skins. Slice into 1-inch pieces. Skewer each variety of vegetable separately for even cooking. Brush with olive oil and sprinkle with salt to taste. Grill on an open or closed grill over medium-hot coals until the vegetables begin browning and are tender when pierced with a skewer. Most root vegetables will cook in approximately 20 minutes.

Mustard Greens Sauce

When selecting mustard greens, look for the smallest, freshest leaves.

> 1 bunch mustard greens
> 2 tablespoons unsalted butter
> 2 shallots, minced
> 2 tablespoons dry sherry
> 1 cup heavy cream or half-and-half
> 1 heaping teaspoon grainy mustard
> 1 heaping teaspoon dried tarragon
> Salt and black pepper, to taste

Wash the mustard greens well in a sink filled with water. Pull off the stems. Chop coarsely and set aside.

Melt the butter in a stainless steel skillet. Cook the shallots over medium heat until they begin softening, about 5 minutes. Add the sherry and chopped mustard greens and cook until the greens are wilted and tender, another 5 minutes. Puree in a blender or food processor.

Over medium heat, combine the cream, mustard, and tarragon and bring just to the boil. Reduce the heat and simmer over low for 15 minutes to thicken the cream. Add the pureed mustard greens, season to taste with salt and pepper, and serve.

Vegetables on the Grill

Serves 4

Tofu is delicious marinated and grilled; it takes on the characteristics of the marinade and grill smoke and becomes crispy and brown on the outside. Plain, steamed short-grain rice is goes well with the tangy flavors of this dish.

Skewered Tofu, Mushrooms, Daikon, and Bok Choy with a Soy, Ginger, and Orange Marinade

Use only tofu labeled "firm" or "extra firm" for grilling, since it holds its shape well while cooking and won't break off the skewers. To drain, pour off the liquid and place the tofu cake between several layers of paper towels. Place a heavy plate on top and drain for 1 to 3 hours.

Soy, Ginger, and Orange Marinade (see below)
One 1-pound package firm tofu, drained
16 to 20 medium-sized *shiitake* mushrooms
1 large daikon radish
1 head bok choy

Prepare the Soy, Ginger, and Orange Marinade. Slice the tofu cake in half lengthwise and marinate for 1 hour at room temperature or longer in the refrigerator, turning frequently.

Wash and trim the mushrooms. Scrub and trim the daikon and slice into 1-inch-thick pieces. Separate the leaves of the bok choy, rinse and pat them dry, and set them aside. Slice the white stems into 1-inch-thick pieces. Marinate the mushrooms, daikon, and bok choy stems for 15 minutes. Slice the tofu into 1-inch cubes.

Brush the bok choy leaves with marinade. To skewer the leaves, fold the sides of each leaf in toward the middle and roll up the leaf, starting at the top. Thread the leaf "packet" onto wooden skewers alternately with the mushrooms, tofu, daikon, and bok choy stem pieces.

On a closed grill over medium-hot coals, grill the skewers for a total of 12 to 15 minutes, turning to cook all sides, or until the mushrooms and tofu are browning and the daikon is tender.

Soy, Ginger, and Orange Marinade

½ cup soy sauce or tamari
½ cup freshly squeezed orange juice
2 tablespoons rice vinegar or cider vinegar
2 tablespoons peanut oil
1 tablespoon dark sesame oil
2 tablespoons minced fresh ginger
¼ teaspoon minced dried hot chili (optional)

Combine all the ingredients and whisk to emulsify.

GRILLED APPETIZERS

*Dry Jack Cheese in Grape-leaf Wrappers · Yam Rounds on Focaccia Squares
Skewered Artichoke Hearts and Cherry Tomatoes · Thin Asparagus with Creamy Lemon Vinaigrette
Grilled Apples and Pears*

Serves 10

Grilled appetizers are perfect for a casual outdoor party, where the guests can capture the delicious snacks hot off the grill. Dry jack is a hard cheese like Parmesan (which can be substituted), with a robust flavor and a less grainy texture. It is produced primarily in Northern California, but is increasingly available across the States. *Focaccia* is an Italian flat bread. See the glossary for information on grilling apples and pears.

Dry Jack Cheese in Grape-leaf Wrappers

Grape leaves come packed in jars and should be drained well and patted dry before using.

> 20 to 30 grape leaves
> Olive oil
> 1 pound dry jack cheese, cut into
>   bite-sized chunks
> Several fresh thyme sprigs

Drain the grape leaves and pat them dry. Lay them flat and brush lightly with olive oil. Place a chunk of cheese and a small pinch of thyme on each leaf and fold into quarters. Oil the outside. Grill this "packet" on an open or covered grill over medium coals for 1 minute per side. The leaves will brown around the edges and the cheese inside will soften. Serve warm.

Yam Rounds on Focaccia Squares

> 3 small yams, sliced into ⅓-inch-thick rounds
> Olive oil
> 1 large *focaccia,* sliced into 2-inch squares
> 1 bunch arugula or watercress, rinsed, drained,
>   and stems removed

Brush the yam slices with olive oil. On an open or covered grill, cook the slices over medium coals until they begin browning and are tender. Serve on *focaccia* squares with a sprig of arugula or watercress.

Skewered Artichoke Hearts and Cherry Tomatoes

> 40 cooked artichoke heart pieces (approximately
>   8 large fresh artichokes or 6 small jars of
>   artichoke hearts packed in oil)
> 20 cherry tomatoes

Thread onto each skewer an artichoke heart, a to-
mato, and another artichoke heart. On an open or closed grill cook over red-hot to medium-hot coals for 10 minutes, turning to cook all sides, until browned.

Thin Asparagus with Creamy Lemon Vinaigrette

> 2 egg yolks
> ⅓ cup lemon juice
> 1 tablespoon Dijon-style mustard
> 1 tablespoon white wine vinegar
> ½ teaspoon salt
> Small pinch of sugar
> 1¾ cups good quality olive oil
> Zest of ½ a lemon
> Freshly ground black pepper to taste
> 2 pounds thin asparagus
> ½ cup butter
> Zest of 1 lemon
> Juice of 1 lemon
> Salt and black pepper to taste

To make the vinaigrette: In a large bowl, whisk together the yolks, lemon juice, mustard, vinegar, salt, and sugar. Begin adding the oil, drop by drop, whisking constantly. When the sauce begins to thicken slightly, add the oil in a thin stream, continuing to whisk vigorously. The dressing should have the consistency of heavy cream. Whisk in the lemon zest and season to taste with pepper. Set aside in the refrigerator.

Rinse the asparagus and peel the tough ends. Melt the butter in a small saucepan and add the zest and juice of the lemon. Add salt and pepper, if desired. Place the asparagus in a shallow dish and coat with butter.

On an open or closed grill over medium-hot coals, grill the asparagus, turning frequently with long-handled tongs. Cook the spears until they are browning and tender, approximately 10 minutes. Serve with Creamy Lemon Vinaigrette.

Vegetables on the Grill

Mango Salsa

Serves 4

Chipotle **chilies are smoked and dried** *jalapeño* **peppers— powerfully hot but with a deep, rich, smoky flavor. This** *chipotle* **sauce, mellowed with yogurt and brown sugar, is less intense, but a little goes a long way. Cool off with delicious Mango Salsa.**

Corn Bread-stuffed Peppers

Use your favorite corn bread recipe, crumble it, and dry it out in a very low oven, or use packaged corn bread stuffing.

> 2 tablespoons oil
> ½ a red onion, thinly sliced
> ½ cup shelled and broken pecans
> 1 small garlic clove, minced
> 1 cup cooked black beans
> 1 tablespoon minced chives
> 1 tablespoon fresh thyme leaves, or 1 teaspoon
>   dried thyme
> 2½ cups crumbled dried corn bread
> ½ to ¾ cup beer
> Salt and freshly ground black pepper, to taste
> 4 large red or yellow bell peppers

Heat the oil in a large skillet over medium heat. Cook the onion until soft, approximately 5 minutes. Add the pecans and garlic and cook for another 3 minutes. Turn off the heat. Add the cooked beans, chives, thyme, and corn bread and toss to combine. Sprinkle the mixture with the beer and toss until lightly moistened. Season to taste with salt and pepper. Set aside.

Cut the tops off the peppers and remove and discard the seeds and whitish core from both the tops and from inside the peppers. Reserve the tops. Stuff the corn bread mixture into the peppers without packing it down. Secure their tops to the peppers with toothpicks. Cook the peppers on a covered grill over a medium-hot to low fire for 1 hour, turning occasionally. Serve with Chipotle Sauce and Mango Salsa.

Chipotle Sauce

Canned *chipotles* usually come packed in a mild red sauce called *adobo*. They are available in the specialty section of most markets. This sauce is not for the faint of heart—it is quite hot but can be toned down by using fewer chilies.

> 3½ ounces canned *chipotle* chilies
>   (half of a 7-ounce can)
> ¼ cup boiling water
> 1½ tablespoons brown sugar
> ¼ teaspoon ground cinnamon
> ¾ cup plain lowfat or nonfat yogurt

Process the chilies, water, brown sugar, and cinnamon in a food processor or blender until smooth. Add the yogurt and pulse several times to combine.

Mango Salsa

Look for a firm, slightly underripe mango. When pomegranates are in season, their seeds make a sweet and colorful addition to this salsa. If arugula is unavailable, use watercress in its place.

> 1 medium-sized mango, peeled, seeded,
>   and diced
> ½ a red onion, chopped
> 3 tablespoons chopped arugula leaves (about
>   1 bunch)
> 1 tablespoon white vinegar
> ¼ cup lime juice (about 2 limes)
> Zest of 1 lime
> 2 tablespoons olive oil
> ½ teaspoon sugar
> Salt and freshly ground pepper to taste

Combine the mango, onion, and arugula leaves in a bowl. Whisk the vinegar, lime juice, zest, olive oil, and sugar together and combine with the mango mixture. Add salt and pepper to taste and let the salsa stand for ½ hour at room temperature or longer in the refrigerator.

Serves 4

This simple grilled sandwich goes well with a cool and refreshing salad of peeled and sliced tangerines, green onion, and mint tossed with a dash of good white wine vinegar and a sprinkle of sugar.

Middle Eastern Eggplant Sandwich with Tahini Dressing

The bread for this sandwich is a flat, slightly leavened loaf. It can also be made on pita bread.

> Tahini Dressing (see below)
> 2 medium-sized eggplants, sliced into
> ¼-inch-thick rounds
> 1 red onion, sliced into ⅓-inch-thick rounds
> Olive oil
> 1 large loaf flat Middle Eastern bread
> 3 hardboiled eggs, sliced
> 2 red ripe tomatoes, sliced
> 1 bunch arugula, sorrel, or watercress
> 8 sprigs Italian parsley

Prepare the Tahini Dressing and set aside.

Brush the eggplant and onion slices with olive oil and grill over medium-hot coals on an open or closed grill for 5 to 7 minutes per side, or until they are browned and tender.

Carefully slice the loaf of bread in half horizontally and spread each half with the Tahini Dressing. Rinse the arugula and parsley and pat dry. Arrange the grilled eggplant, onion, hardboiled egg, tomato slices, arugula leaves, and parsley sprigs on one half, top with the other half, and slice the sandwich into serving-sized pieces.

Tahini Dressing

Tahini is a paste made from sesame seeds. It is widely used in Middle Eastern cooking, and its nutty, earthy taste is quite distinctive. Stir it well before using. This dressing makes a delicious dip or sauce for grilled vegetables.

> ¾ cup tahini
> 1 garlic clove, minced to a paste
> ½ teaspoon salt
> Juice of ½ a lemon
> 3 tablespoons water

Combine all the ingredients and mix well.

Vegetables on the Grill

Three-grain Rice

Serves 6

Choose a basketful of the freshest seasonal vegetables for this simple dish of grilled vegetables and sauces with rice.

Vegetable Medley with Three Dipping Sauces

> Curry-Ginger Sauce (see below)
> Poppyseed-Orange Vinaigrette (see below)
> Aïoli with Basil (see below)
> 1½ pounds assorted vegetables
> Olive oil

Prepare the sauces and set aside.

Wash and stem the vegetables; slice into halves or chunks or leave whole if they are small. Brush the vegetables with olive oil. Skewer the vegetables or place them all in a hinged wire grill basket. On a covered grill over medium-hot coals, cook the vegetables according to the timetables suggested in the glossary for each variety, or until browned and tender when pierced with a skewer. Most vegetables cook in 10 to 15 minutes. Serve the vegetables with Three-grain Rice and the sauces for dipping.

Curry-Ginger Sauce

> 1 cup plain lowfat or nonfat yogurt
> 1 tablespoon curry powder
> ¼ teaspoon powdered ginger
> 1 green onion, white part and half the green leaves, minced
> Pinch of sugar
> Salt, to taste

Combine all the ingredients.

Poppyseed-Orange Vinaigrette

> ½ cup olive oil
> ¼ cup freshly squeezed orange juice
> Grated zest of ¼ orange
> 1 tablespoon poppy seeds
> Small pinch of sugar
> Salt and freshly ground black pepper, to taste

Whisk all the ingredients together until they are emulsified.

Aïoli with Basil

> 2 egg yolks
> 1 tablespoon white wine vinegar
> 1 tablespoon lemon juice
> ¼ teaspoon salt
> 1 to 1¼ cups fruity olive oil
> 1 scant tablespoon boiling water
> 2 garlic cloves, minced to a paste
> 1 heaping tablespoon chopped fresh basil leaves, or 1 teaspoon dried basil
> Grated zest of ½ a lemon
> Pinch of sugar
> Salt and freshly ground pepper, to taste

In a large bowl, whisk together the yolks, vinegar, lemon juice, and salt. Add the oil drop by drop, whisking constantly. When the mixture begins to thicken, add the oil in a thin stream, whisking vigorously. If the mayonnaise begins to separate, stop the flow of oil and whisk until the sauce coalesces. When the mayonnaise is the desired thickness, whisk in the boiling water to set it. Whisk in the garlic, basil, lemon zest, sugar, and season to taste.

Three-grain Rice

Wehani rice is a russet-colored variety of long grain brown rice developed by the Lundbergs, the same California farmers who first grew organic rice commercially. The nutritious layers of bran and germ are intact on the grain, and it has a nutty aroma as it cooks. Wehani can be found in some supermarkets, or in health food stores.

> ½ cup brown rice
> ½ cup Wehani rice
> ½ cup rye berries or wheat berries
> 2¾ cups water or vegetable broth
> ½ teaspoon salt

Rinse the rice and rye berries in a sieve under running water. Put the washed grains in a large pot with the water and salt. Bring to a boil. Stir once, reduce the heat, and cover with a tight-fitting lid. Cook over very low heat for 35 to 40 minutes, or until the grains are tender. Let the rice stand, covered, for 10 minutes before serving.

Summer Salad with Quinoa

Serves 6

In this late spring or early summer salad grilled vegetables are combined with fresh spinach and quinoa, an ancient grain from South America that is known for its high-quality protein content.

Vegetable suggestions are listed below, but substitute those that are freshest in the market if necessary. If the mood strikes, this is also an opportunity to grill a slice or two of fruit to add a hint of mellow sweetness to the salad.

> Lemon-Mustard Vinaigrette (see below)
> ½ bunch fresh spinach
> 1 bunch curly endive *(frisée)*
> 1 cup quinoa
> 2 cups water
> ¼ teaspoon salt
> Summer squashes (crookneck, zucchini, pattypan)
> Carrots
> Bell peppers
> New potatoes
> Belgian endive
> Pineapple
> Avocado for garnish
> Cherry tomatoes for garnish

Prepare the Lemon-Mustard Vinaigrette and set aside. Wash the spinach carefully in a sink filled with water, changing the water once to get all the grit off the leaves. Pull off the stems. Wash the curly endive. Pat or spin dry both the spinach and the endive. Tear into pieces and set aside in the refrigerator.

Rinse the quinoa thoroughly in a sieve under cold running water, tossing it a few times to make sure all the grains are rinsed. Bring the water to a boil, add the salt, and stir in the quinoa. Reduce the heat and simmer, covered, for 20 minutes. The grain, when cooked, should not be mushy, and the tiny spiral of the germ will be visible. Fluff the grain with a fork and set aside to cool.

Wash and slice the vegetables and fruit (except the avocado and cherry tomatoes) into bite-sized chunks and skewer. Use some of the vinaigrette as a light baste. Grill the vegetable skewers until browned and tender, approximately 15 minutes for everything.

Toss the quinoa, spinach, and curly endive together with just enough vinaigrette to moisten the leaves lightly. Toss again with the grilled vegetables and serve immediately, garnished with chunks of avocado and cherry tomatoes.

Lemon-Mustard Vinaigrette

This vinaigrette is used both to dress the salad and to baste the vegetables for the grill.

> Grated zest of 1 lemon
> 2 tablespoons lemon juice
> 2 teaspoons Dijon-style mustard
> ¼ cup olive oil
> Salt and freshly ground black pepper, to taste

Combine the zest, lemon juice, and mustard in a bowl. Whisk in the olive oil until emulsified. Season to taste with salt and pepper.

Vegetables on the Grill

Serves 4

These hearty corn pancakes are more like individual round corn breads. With roasted vegetables and a light citrus sauce, they become part of a savory dish rather than being breakfast fare. A simple salad of mixed varieties of lettuce rounds out this filling meal.

Corn Cakes with Roasted Vegetables

Make the corn pancakes ahead and reheat them on the grill before serving.

The elephant garlic can be roasting as the grill is heating up and while you make the corn cakes. Place it away from the hottest part of the fire.

> Orange Cream Sauce (see below)
> 1 head elephant garlic, or 1 head garlic
> 1 tablespoon olive oil
> 4 Corn Cakes (see below)
> 6 tablespoons butter
> 1 heaping tablespoon fresh thyme leaves,
>   or 1 teaspoon dried thyme
> 1 tablespoon olive oil
> 1 red bell pepper, sliced into large chunks
> 4 zucchini, sliced into chunks
> 4 pattypan squash, sliced into chunks
> 4 green onions

Prepare the Orange Cream Sauce and set aside in the refrigerator.

From heavy-duty aluminum foil make a baking cup large enough to accommodate the head of elephant garlic. Peel away some the papery layers from the head, place it in the cup, drizzle olive oil over the top, and place it away from the hottest part of the fire. Cover the grill and cook the garlic for 45 minutes, or until tender.

Prepare the corn cakes and set aside, loosely covered with foil.

Melt the butter in a small saucepan, add the thyme, and brush all the vegetable chunks with it. Skewer the vegetables or arrange them in a hinged grill basket. Grill the green onions whole. Cook the vegetables on a covered grill over medium-hot coals until tender and browning.

Brush the corn cakes with the remaining melted butter and warm them quickly on the grill. Distribute the vegetables and roasted garlic on the corn cakes and serve with Orange Cream Sauce.

Orange Cream Sauce

> 1 cup sour cream
> 2 tablespoons freshly squeezed orange juice
> 2 tablespoons orange zest

Combine the ingredients in a bowl and set aside in the refrigerator.

Corn Cakes

These are hearty cornmeal pancakes made with both regular and coarse cornmeal. This recipe makes 4 large cakes.

> 2 cups milk
> 1 cup yellow cornmeal
> ¼ cup coarse cornmeal
> 2 eggs
> 2 tablespoons honey
> 3 tablespoons melted butter
> 1¼ cups unbleached flour
> 2 teaspoons baking powder
> ½ teaspoon baking soda
> ½ teaspoon salt
> Butter

Pour the milk over the regular and coarse cornmeal in a large bowl. Set aside to soak for 5 minutes.

Beat the eggs, honey, and melted butter together. Stir into the cornmeal. Sift the flour, baking powder, baking soda, and salt together and add to the cornmeal, stirring just enough to moisten.

Heat a well-seasoned griddle or nonstick skillet over medium heat. Melt ¼ tablespoon butter to keep the corn cakes from sticking, if necessary.

To make each corn cake, drop 1 cupful of batter onto a prepared griddle or skillet. Cook until bubbles appear and break on the top, turn, and cook for another few minutes until done. Set aside on a plate, covered loosely with foil.

Hot off the Grill

Serves 6

Begin this Indian-style meal with *pappadums*—spicy lentil wafers that crisp on the grill in seconds. They are delicious eaten as is or dipped in a cool relish of chopped cucumbers in yogurt and mint or a spicy salsa. A *basmati* rice pilaf made with sweet peas and saffron is a nice mild backdrop for the rich Almond-Spice Sauce.

Vegetables with Northern Indian Almond-Spice Sauce

Cook the vegetables separately on metal skewers or all together in a hinged wire grill basket.

½ cup vegetable oil
2 teaspoons black mustard seeds
1 small fresh hot green chili, sliced into rings
Northern Indian Almond-Spice Sauce
  (see below)
½ winter squash, sliced into chunks
1 small cauliflower, separated into florets
4 medium-sized carrots, sliced into chunks
3 potatoes, sliced into chunks

In a small saucepan, combine the oil, mustard seeds, and green chilies and heat over very low heat for 10 minutes. Set aside to cool. This oil baste can be prepared several days in advance. The longer it stands the hotter it will be.

Prepare the Almond-Spice Sauce and set aside.

Steam the squash chunks until just barely tender, approximately 5 minutes. Brush the squash, cauliflower, carrot, and potato chunks with the chili oil and arrange in a grill basket or on metal skewers. On a covered grill over medium-hot coals, cook the vegetables for 10 to 12 minutes per side, or until they are tender when pierced with a skewer and are browning. Serve with Almond-Spice Sauce.

Northern Indian Almond-Spice Sauce

Garam masala is a blend of dry spices characteristic of northern Indian cuisine. It is milder than curry, but with a complex flavor dominated by coriander, cumin, and cardamom.

4 tablespoons butter
1 tablespoon ground coriander
½ teaspoon ground cumin
¼ cup ground blanched almonds
¼ teaspoon ground ginger
1 small garlic clove, minced
1 cup plain lowfat yogurt
½ tablespoon tomato paste mixed with
  1 tablespoon water
1 tablespoon *garam masala*
2 tablespoons minced fresh cilantro
Salt, to taste

Heat the butter in a heavy saucepan over medium heat. Add the coriander and cumin, then the almonds, ginger, and garlic and cook for 2 minutes. Reduce the heat. Add the yogurt and tomato paste and water mixture, stirring well, and simmer gently for 10 minutes. Stir in the *garam masala* and cilantro and simmer for another minute. Season with salt to taste. Reheat gently over very low heat and serve warm.

Vegetables on the Grill

Serves 6

Portobello mushrooms are becoming more common in the supermarket. They are quite large and meaty, with a deep brown flesh and a spreading cap. Portobellos have a depth of flavor reminiscent of *porcini* mushrooms, with the advantage that they are cultivated rather than harvested in the wild and are thus more available. If Portobellos are not available, large oyster mushrooms make a delicious substitute.

Garlicky Portobello Mushrooms

Portobellos have an open cap, so the indicators of freshness are an even color and a dry, firm feel. Use them within a day or so of purchase, as they perish quickly. Store them in a single layer, if possible, loosely covered with a damp paper towel. Do not enclose them in a plastic bag. Wash them only *just* before using them, and avoid running too much water on the spongy undersides. Carefully pat them dry with paper towels.

> 3 tablespoons butter
> 4 tablespoons olive oil
> 1 tablespoon lemon juice
> 3 garlic cloves, minced
> Freshly ground black pepper
> 8 to 12 large fresh Portobello mushrooms, washed and stems removed

Melt the butter, olive oil, lemon juice, garlic, and pepper together in a small saucepan (you can do this on the grill). Slice any mushrooms that are over 3 inches in diameter into strips. Brush the mushrooms generously with the butter baste. On a covered grill over medium-hot coals, grill the mushrooms undersides down, for approximately 8 minutes, turn, and grill the tops for 8 more minutes. The mushrooms should be very tender when pierced with a skewer and very well browned.

Spaghetti with Piquant Green Sauce

This flavorful sauce can also be used on grilled vegetables or polenta.

> 1 cup well-packed Italian parsley leaves
> 3 tablespoons drained capers
> 1 large garlic clove, sliced
> 1 hardboiled egg, yolk only
> 2 tablespoons red wine vinegar
> ½ cup extra virgin olive oil
> Salt to taste
> 1½ pounds spaghetti
> 1 tablespoon salt
> Parmesan cheese

Combine the parsley, capers, garlic, egg yolk, and vinegar in a food processor and process until minced. With the processor running, add the oil in a thin stream until it is entirely incorporated. Season with salt.

Cook the spaghetti in 6 quarts of boiling salted water until *al dente*. Drain, leaving some moisture clinging to the noodles, and immediately turn into a warm serving bowl. Toss with the sauce and serve immediately with Parmesan cheese.

Vegetables on the Grill

Serves 4

Grilling it gives polenta an earthy and delicious roasted corn flavor; the outside becomes crispy while the inside is almost puddinglike. Prepare the polenta and, while it is cooling, light the grill and make the Salsa Cruda.

Basil and Pine Nut Polenta

The basil and toasted pine nuts in this polenta provide a variation on the traditional version.

⅓ cup pine nuts
8 large fresh basil leaves
4⅓ cups water
1 teaspoon salt
1 cup polenta or coarsely ground cornmeal
2 tablespoons butter
Olive oil

Toast the pine nuts in a preheated 375° oven until light brown, about 4 minutes. Rinse the basil leaves and pat dry. Do not chop the leaves until just before adding them to the polenta.

Bring the water to a boil in a large, heavy saucepan and add the salt. Add the polenta very slowly, stirring constantly with a wooden spoon to prevent lumps. Reduce the heat and cook over low heat, stirring frequently, for 25 to 35 minutes. As the polenta thickens, press out any lumps on the side of the pan. The polenta is done when it pulls away from the side of the pan.

To the cooked polenta add the butter and toasted pine nuts. Sliver the basil leaves and add them also. Spread the polenta into a buttered 8-inch square or 10-inch round pan or dish. Cool for an hour or more.

Slice the polenta into wedges and brush with olive oil. On an open or closed grill over medium-hot coals, grill the polenta slices until lightly browned and heated through, approximately 10 minutes per side. Serve with Salsa Cruda.

Salsa Cruda

To peel tomatoes easily, drop them into a pot of simmering water for 20 seconds and promptly remove. The skins will slip right off.

3 large red ripe tomatoes, peeled, seeded, and finely chopped (1½ to 2 pounds)
2 tablespoons drained capers
1 large garlic clove, minced to a paste or put through a garlic press
8 fresh basil leaves, slivered
3 tablespoons minced Italian parsley
2 tablespoons extra virgin olive oil
Dash balsamic vinegar
3 tablespoons freshly grated *pecorino* cheese (or Parmesan cheese)
Pinch of sugar
Salt and freshly ground pepper, to taste
¼ teaspoon finely minced dried red chili pepper (optional)

In a large glass bowl, mix all the ingredients together with a wooden spoon. Let stand, covered, at room temperature for 1 hour, or longer in the refrigerator.

Hot off the Grill

Serves 6

Tempeh is a wonderfully versatile soy product that merits attention. This ancient Indonesian food is a fermented soy cake made of split soy beans, which give it a heartier flavor and texture than tofu. It is very high in protein—it has about twice as much as a hamburger. It is delicious grilled since it absorbs marinade flavors easily, as well as the delicious savor of grill smoke. Tempeh cakes are often mixed with other grains, such as brown rice or quinoa. These varieties are more flavorful than plain tempeh.

Grilled Tempeh with Red Onion and Eggplant on Whole Wheat Toast

Eggplant slices can be salted and allowed to drain for half an hour to rid them of any bitterness. See page 38 for more information.

> Red Wine Marinade (see below)
> 3 tempeh cakes
> Sweet Lemon Mayonnaise (see below)
> 1 large red onion, sliced into 6 rounds
> 2 small eggplants, sliced into ⅓-inch-thick rounds
> Olive oil
> 12 slices whole wheat bread
> 1 bunch arugula

Prepare the Red Wine Marinade. Slice the tempeh cakes in half crosswise, then split each half horizontally by slicing carefully. Marinate the tempeh cakes at room temperature for 1 hour, or longer in the refrigerator.

Prepare the Sweet Lemon Mayonnaise and set aside in the refrigerator.

Brush the eggplant slices with olive oil. On an open or closed grill over medium-hot coals, grill the eggplant and onion slices for 10 minutes per side and the tempeh for 8 minutes per side or until well-browned. Grill the whole wheat bread slices over low coals until toasty. Arrange the vegetables and tempeh on slices of whole wheat toast spread with Sweet Lemon Mayonnaise and several sprigs of fresh arugula.

Red Wine Marinade

Tempeh readily takes on assertive flavors such as wine, garlic, rosemary, and fennel. It also combines well with soy sauce, vinegars, ginger, and citrus juice, which makes it very versatile indeed.

> 1 cup red wine
> 4 tablespoons olive oil
> 2 large garlic cloves, sliced into ovals
> 1 tablespoon rosemary leaves, or 1 teaspoon dried rosemary
> ¼ teaspoon fennel seeds
> Coarsely ground black pepper

Combine all the ingredients.

Sweet Lemon Mayonnaise

> ½ cup mayonnaise
> 2 tablespoons lemon juice
> 1 teaspoon Dijon-style mustard
> 1 teaspoon honey
> 1 garlic clove, minced to a paste
> Salt and freshly ground pepper, to taste

Combine all the ingredients.

Hot off the Grill

Grilled Artichokes

Eggplant, New Potato, and Fennel with Sour Cream Sauce

Select firm, fresh eggplant the day it is needed, if possible. Look for fennel with the stalks and feathery leaves attached, since the leaves can be sprinkled on the salad.

> 2 medium-sized eggplants
> Sour Cream Sauce (see below)
> 16 to 20 new potatoes
> 2 fennel bulbs
> Olive oil

Slice the eggplant into ⅓-inch-thick rounds. Arrange in one layer on paper towels and sprinkle with salt. Allow the eggplant to drain for half an hour. Meanwhile, prepare the Sour Cream Sauce and set aside in the refrigerator.

Skewer the new potatoes on metal skewers. Trim the fennel bulbs, reserving some of the feathery leaves, if available. Cut each bulb into quarters or sixths and skewer. Brush the potatoes and fennel with olive oil and grill, covered, over medium-hot coals for 20 to 25 minutes.

Meanwhile, pat the eggplant slices to remove the salt and excess moisture. Brush with olive oil and grill the slices over medium-hot coals for 12 to 15 minutes. All the vegetables should be brown and tender when pierced with a skewer.

Slice the grilled fennel into thin strips. Arrange all the vegetables on a platter and drizzle with the Sour Cream Sauce. Sprinkle fennel leaves on top.

Sour Cream Sauce

The slight hint of garlic in this sauce is just right for the combination of vegetables.

> ½ cup olive oil
> 2 tablespoons rice wine vinegar
> 1 teaspoon Dijon-style mustard
> 2 teaspoons lemon juice
> 2 heaping tablespoons sour cream
> 1 garlic clove, minced to a paste
> Small pinch of sugar
> Salt and pepper, to taste

Whisk the olive oil, vinegar, mustard, and lemon juice together until emulsified. Whisk in the sour cream. Add the garlic and sugar and season to taste with salt and pepper. Set aside in the refrigerator until needed.

Grilled Artichokes

Start these on a cooler side of the grill just when the coals have started up—they'll take almost an hour on the grill but are well worth it.

> 2 fresh artichokes
> 1 lemon
> 2 cloves garlic, coarsely chopped
> 4 tablespoons olive oil
> 8 tablespoons water

Trim off the stems and the spiny tips of the artichoke leaves, slice the artichokes in half lengthwise, and rinse them well under running water. Scrape out the choke. Using half a lemon for each artichoke, squeeze lemon juice all over the cut sides.

From heavy-duty aluminum foil, fashion thick baking cups large enough to accommodate each artichoke half with extra foil to bend over the top. Place an artichoke half in each cup, cut-side up, sprinkle with chopped garlic, and drizzle a tablespoon of olive oil over each one. Sprinkle with salt and pepper. Add 2 tablespoons of water to each cup and bend the top edges inward to cover the artichoke halves amost completely. On a closed grill over medium-hot coals, grill the artichokes for 1 hour, or until tender when pierced with a skewer.

Serves 4

Classic Thai *satay* is made of thinly sliced and marinated beef, pork, or chicken grilled and served with a delicious peanut sauce. This tofu *satay* is marinated in a combination of typical Thai ingredients that are not common on our grocery shelves. *Nam pla,* a Thai condiment made of salted fish, is an essential ingredient in Thai cuisine. It is saltier than soy sauce (which can be substituted), but milder, despite its pungent odor. It mellows when cooked and adds a natural smoky flavor to foods.

Tofu Satay with Tangy Dipping Sauce

Buy only "firm" or "extra firm" tofu.

> 2 pounds firm tofu
> Satay Sauce (see below)
> Tangy Dipping Sauce (see below)
> 4 tablespoons peanut or vegetable oil
> 2 tablespoons dry sherry
> 1 tablespoon chopped fresh lemongrass
>   (the tender inner stalks) or
>   1½ tablespoons dried lemongrass
> 2 garlic cloves
> 1 tablespoon curry powder
> ½ teaspoon minced dried red chili pepper
> 2 teaspoons brown sugar

Drain the liquid from the tofu and place the cakes between several layers of paper towels. Weight the top with a heavy plate and drain for 1 to 3 hours. While the tofu is draining, prepare the Satay and Tangy Dipping Sauces. When the tofu is drained, slice each cake lengthwise into 4 strips.

In a food processor or blender combine the oil, sherry, lemongrass, garlic, curry powder, chili pepper, and brown sugar, and process until smooth. Pour this mixture over the tofu strips, toss gently to coat the pieces, and marinate for 1 hour, or longer in the refrigerator.

Soak 16 wooden skewers in water for 15 minutes. Carefully insert two skewers parallel and about one inch apart lengthwise into each tofu slice. Oil the grill. On a closed grill over medium-hot coals, grill the tofu, turning once, until browned, 10 to 12 minutes total. Serve with Satay Sauce and Tangy Dipping Sauce.

Satay Sauce

> 2 tablespoons peanut or vegetable oil
> ½ a medium-sized white onion, minced
> 1 garlic clove, minced
> 2 teaspoons curry powder
> 1 cup canned coconut milk
> 1 tablespoon *nam pla*
> 1 tablespoon brown sugar
> ½ teaspoon minced dried red chili pepper
> 1 tablespoon minced fresh lemongrass
>   (the tender inner stalks)
> ½ cup unsalted crunchy peanut butter

Heat the oil in a small skillet over medium-high heat. Cook the onion and garlic until the onion is wilting, approximately 2 minutes. Add the curry powder and cook for another 30 seconds. Add the coconut milk, *nam pla,* brown sugar, dried chili pepper, lemongrass, and peanut butter. Cook over very low heat, stirring frequently, for 5 minutes, or until slightly thickened.

Tangy Dipping Sauce

> 2 tablespoons sugar
> ¼ cup water
> 3 tablespoons white or red wine vinegar
> ½ tablespoon *nam pla*
> ¼ teaspoon dried red chili flakes
> 2 tablespoons grated carrot
> 1 tablespoon chopped roasted peanuts

In a small saucepan over low heat, dissolve the sugar in the water. Remove from heat and stir in the vinegar, *nam pla,* and dried chili flakes. When completely cool, add the carrot and peanuts and serve.

GRILL COCKTAIL PARTY

Serves 8

Each plate of grilled appetizers is a composition of delectable savory flavors, beautiful to look at but better to eat. Cloves of the roasted whole heads of garlic can be squeezed onto a flavorful coarse-grained bread lightly toasted on the grill. Olives, preferably the kind you find in ethnic markets, such as Kalamatas, Niçoise, green Cevinols, and the tiny black wrinkled olives from Morocco, add a salty bite. A grilled Japanese eggplant half is sweet and smoky—delicious on the bread or as is. Belgian endive can be sliced and eaten, or the leaves used to scoop up small bites of tangy goat cheese.

There are many options for a "grilled nibbles" plate. Any variety of baby vegetable can be skewered, brushed with oil and lightly salted, and grilled over the coals. Slices of summer squash are delicious as well. Try also any variety of mushroom grilled and served with a light garlicky sauce, or skewered cherry tomatoes and baby corn.

Grilled Japanese Eggplant

> 4 Japanese eggplants
> Olive oil

Slice the eggplants in half lengthwise. Brush with olive oil and grill over medium-hot coals for approximately 5 minutes per side, or until they are browning and tender when pierced with a skewer.

Grilled Belgian Endive

> 4 Belgian endives
> Olive oil

Slice the endives in half lengthwise. Brush with olive oil and grill over medium-hot coals for 7 to 8 minutes per side, or until they are browning and tender when pierced with a skewer.

Roasted Whole Heads of Garlic

Look for firm garlic heads with securely attached cloves.

> 8 whole garlic heads
> ½ cup olive oil
> Several sprigs fresh rosemary
> Salt and freshly ground black pepper

Peel away some of the papery layers from the garlic heads, particularly from down among the top cloves, taking care not to break off the cloves. Slice off the tops. From 8 squares of heavy aluminum foil, form 8 muffin-sized cups, making sure that they are pinched together firmly so that they will not leak.

Place the garlic heads in the cups and drizzle 1 tablespoon of olive oil over the top of each, allowing it to run down in between the cloves and into the bottom of the cup. Sprinkle with rosemary leaves, salt, and pepper. On a covered grill, away from the hottest coals, cook the garlic for 1 hour, using a baster to drizzle on more olive oil once or twice while it cooks. Garlic is done when the cloves are browned and mushy.

Toasted Bread Slices

Any bread with a "toothy" grain—not the French breads that are very soft—is a good candidate for the grill. Cut the bread into ½-inch slices and lightly toast it over medium-hot to low coals. It burns quickly, so watch carefully. For *bruschetta*, the Italian garlic bread, dip one toasted side into olive oil (it works best to have the oil poured out onto a plate) and then rub that side lightly with a raw garlic clove.

Vegetables on the Grill

Serves 4 to 6

Grill-cooked pizzas flavored with the smoke of hardwood are reminiscent of the authentic Italian pizzas cooked in a wood-fired oven. Look for hardwood chunks, often sold in gourmet or bar-becue stores or available by mail order. Light the hardwood chunks at the same time as the charcoal; there is no need to soak them in advance. They will burn down to glowing embers a little more slowly than the charcoal, but will make a nice hot fire with sweet-smelling smoke, perfect for pizzas. Use 6 to 8 chunks with the charcoal.

Four toppings are suggested for you to choose from, though the recipe is only for two large pizzas. If you cook more than two, you may need to add hot coals to the grill to maintain the high temperature necessary for successful pizza cooking. Pizza stones are available in most gourmet cookware stores.

Wood-smoked Pizzas

This recipe makes enough dough for two 12- to 15-inch pizzas.

2 packages active dry yeast
½ teaspoon sugar
1 cup lukewarm water
3 tablespoons olive oil
1 teaspoon salt
3¾ cups unbleached all-purpose flour

In a large bowl combine the yeast and sugar in the lukewarm water. Let the mixture stand for about 10 minutes, or until the yeast begins to foam. Add the olive oil, salt, and 3½ cups of the flour, and blend into dough. Turn the dough out onto a floured surface and knead, incorporating as much as possible of the remaining ¼ cup flour. Continue kneading the dough until it is smooth and elastic, about 10 minutes. Put the dough into an oiled bowl, turn it to coat with oil, cover with a kitchen towel, and let it rise in a warm place for 2½ to 3 hours, or until doubled in bulk. Punch the dough down. Divide the dough into two balls. On a floured surface press each ball into a 12- to 15-inch round, leaving it a little thicker at the edge to hold the topping.

Place a pizza stone on a covered grill with red-hot coals (you want the flames to have subsided) to preheat it. Put the dough on a very well floured surface so that the pizza can easily be slid from it onto the stone. Assemble each pizza with its topping. Place the pizza on the stone and cook, covered, for 10 to 15 minutes, or until the dough is golden brown and the topping bubbly.

Garlic and Mushroom Topping

6 to 8 large garlic cloves
½ cup olive oil
4 to 6 large oyster mushrooms, or 1 dozen smaller mushrooms
2 tablespoons fresh rosemary leaves, or 3 teaspoons dried rosemary
⅓ cup grated Parmesan cheese

Peel the garlic cloves. Cook over low heat in the olive oil until golden, approximately 30 minutes. Remove and allow to cool, reserving the oil. Thinly slice the garlic cloves. Clean the mushrooms and slice them into strips. Using 2 tablespoons of the garlic cooking oil, sauté the mushrooms in a large skillet over high heat until they just begin to color, about 5 minutes. Brush the pizza dough liberally with the garlic cooking oil, distribute the garlic, rosemary, and mushrooms, in that order, over the dough. Sprinkle with Parmesan and grill, according to the instructions outlined above, for approximately 15 minutes.

Eggplant and Goat Cheese Topping

3 Japanese eggplants, or 1 medium-sized eggplant
Olive oil
4 ounces *chèvre*
10 basil leaves

Trim and slice the eggplant lengthwise into ¼-inch-thick slices (slice regular eggplant into rounds). Brush with olive oil and grill until browning. Do this while the grill is heating up, but on a cooler part of the grill. Brush the dough with olive oil, arrange the eggplant slices, crumbled *chèvre,* and basil leaves on top. Grill, according to the instructions outlined above, for approximately 15 minutes.

Vegetables on the Grill

Fennel and Tomato Topping

2 medium-sized fennel bulbs, sliced into strips
1 tablespoon olive oil
1 tablespoon butter
4 yellow and red plum tomatoes, thinly sliced
1 cup grated mozzarella cheese

Trim the fennel bulbs and slice them into strips. Heat the olive oil and butter in a large skillet over medium-high heat. Sauté the fennel until soft and browning, approximately 10 minutes. Brush the dough with olive oil and arrange the tomato slices, fennel, and mozzarella over the pizza dough. Grill, according to the instructions outlined above, for approximately 15 minutes.

Sun-dried Tomato and Olive Topping

Reconstitute sun-dried tomatoes by soaking them in hot water for 15 minutes to half an hour, or use the type packed in oil and drain them on paper towels before slicing them. Also, for this recipe, roast the red pepper ahead or use the variety packed in oil and drain well.

Olive oil
15 to 20 thinly sliced, reconstituted sun-dried tomatoes
12 small green or black Greek olives
1 large red pepper, roasted, peeled, and sliced into strips
2 tablespoons drained capers
1 cup grated Fontina cheese

Brush the pizza dough with olive oil. Distribute the tomato strips, olives, red pepper, and capers evenly over the dough. Sprinkle the grated cheese on top. Grill, according to the instructions outlined above, for approximately 15 minutes.

Grill Manufacturers

Check with any of these grill manufacturers for mail order information or for a distributor near you.

Char-Broil

W.C. Bradley Enterprises
P.O. Box 1300
Columbus, GA 31993
(800) 241-8981
All sizes of charcoal and gas grills, smokers, and a wide range of accessories.

Charmglow

500 S. Madison
Duquoin, IL 62832
(618) 542-4781
All sizes of outdoor gas grills, smokers, and gas grill accessories.

Ducane

800 Dutch Square Boulevard
Columbia, SC 29210-7376
(803) 798-1600
All sizes of outdoor gas grills.

The Grillery

Grillworks, Inc.
1211 Ferdon Road
Ann Arbor, MI 48104
(313) 995-2164
Gourmet wood cooker for outdoors and fireplace.

Hasty-Bake

7656 E. 46th Street
Tulsa, OK 74145
(800) 4AN-OVEN
Gourmet charcoal cookers of all sizes.

Kamado

BSW, Inc.
4680 E. Second Street
Benicia, CA 94510
(707) 745-8175
Traditional Japanese earthenware oven/barbecue/smoker.

Kingsford/Clorox Company

1221 Broadway
Oakland, CA 94612
(800) 537-2823
Charcoal grills, charcoal, charcoal chimneys.

Tuscan Grill

Smith & Hawkin
(415) 383-4415
Adjustable wrought-iron fireplace grill.

Weber

Weber-Stephens Products Company
200 E. Daniels Road
Palatine, IL 60067
(800) 323-7598
All sizes of charcoal kettles and gas grills and accessories.

Fuel Sources

These charcoal and wood chip and chunk distributors will sell by mail order or will direct you to their nearest retailers.

Connecticut Charcoal Company

Old Time Charcoal
(203) 684-3208
Pure hardwood charcoal.

Lazzari Fuel Company

P.O. Box 34051
San Francisco, CA 94034
(415) 467-2970 (within California)
(800) 242-7265 (outside California)
Pure mesquite charcoal. Many varieties of wood chips and chunks.

Tool Sources

Call these tool manufacturers and distributors for a retailer in your area.

Charcoal Companion

7955 Edgewater Dr.
Oakland, CA 94621
(415) 632-2100
Chimneys and many other grill tools.

Griffo-Grill Inc.

1400 N. 30th Street
Quincy, IL 62301
(800) 426-1286
All sizes of high-quality stainless steel grill racks and hinged grill baskets.

Outdoor Chef

P.O. Box 6255
Evansville, IN 47719-0255
(800) 544-5362
All types of tools, equipment, and parts for charcoal and gas grills.

Weber

Weber-Stephens Products Company
200 E. Daniels Road
Palatine, Il 60067
(800) 323-7598
Equipment for Weber grills and all types of grilling tools.

Grill Book
List of Menus

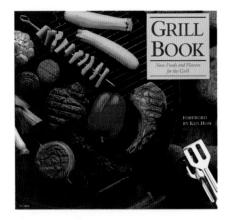

Butterflied Leg of Lamb with Zinfandel Sauce

Veal Chops with Gruyère and Prosciutto

Skewered Scallops, Zucchini, and Artichoke Hearts with Salsa

Grilled Whole Trout

Grilled Steak with Fresh Herbs

Salmon Steaks with Chive Butter

Tofu Marinated in Sesame Oil and Rice Vinegar with Scallions

Rock Cornish Game Hens in Raspberry Vinegar Marinade

Sesame Flank Steak

Boneless Pork Loin in Sherry Vinegar, Port, and Prune Marinade

Grilled Split Lobster Tail

Mixed Sausage Grill

Chicken Breasts in Many Mustards

Nam Prik Shrimp

Grilled Breast of Duck in Red Wine Marinade

Peanut Chicken on Skewers

Barbecued Baby Back Ribs in Honey, Tamari, and Orange Marinade

Grill Appetizer Party

The Art of Grilling
List of Menus

Grilled Italian Appetizers

Tandoori Chicken

Rack of Lamb with Port, Rosemary, and Garlic Marinade

Soft-shell Crab with Hazelnut Butter

Burgers and Red Onion Slices

Boneless Quail with Corn Bread and Escarole Stuffing

Peppers Stuffed with Eggplant

Prawns with Spicy Remoulade

Tenderloin of Beef with Mustard-Mint Sauce

Calves' Liver with Sage Butter and Pancetta

Lime-marinated Rock Cornish Game Hens

Ham Steak with Apple Cream Sauce

Grapevine-smoked Salmon, Trout, and Oysters

Veal Roast with Marsala and Dried Apricots

Hickory-grilled Pork Chops with Fresh Peaches

Rabbit with Pecan Butter and Apples

Monkfish with Caper Vinaigrette

Steak Teriyaki Rice Bowl

Thai Barbecued Chicken

Spiedini with Balsamic Marinade

Swordfish with Pico de Gallo

Turkey Breast Smoked with Cherry Wood

Sea Bass on Bok Choy with Ginger-Garlic Butter

Hickory-smoked Country-style Ribs with Barbecue Sauce

A

Adobo, 65
Aïoli, with basil, 69
Aluminum foil, uses
    for, in grilling, 16
Anise, sweet. *See* Fennel
Appetizers, grilled, 62,
    86
Apples,
    to grill, 25
    grilled, with pecan
        nut butter, 53
Apricot, to grill, 25–26
Art of Grilling, The,
    contents of, 92
Artichokes,
    globe,
        to grill, 26
        grilled, 57, 83
        hearts of, grilled,
            with tomatoes,
            62
    Jerusalem,
        to grill, 30
        grilled, 58
Arugula, 65, 66, 81
Asparagus,
    to grill, 26
    grilled, 44, 62
Aubergine. *See*
    Eggplant
Avocado, 50, 70

B

Baking cups, to make of
    aluminum foil, 16
Banana, to grill, 27
Basil,
    in *aïoli,* 69
    with noodles, 44
    in polenta, 79
    in salsa, 79
Basket. *See* Grill basket
Baste, butter, 21, 53
Basting, sauce for, 21
Bean,
    asparagus. *See* Bean,
        yard-long

black,
    and corn, 43
    in corn-bread
        stuffing, 65
Chinese long. *See*
    Bean, yard-long
    yam. *See Jícama*
yard-long (asparagus
    bean, Chinese long
    bean), to grill, 39
Bean curd. *See* Tofu
Beets,
    to grill, 27
    grilled, 57, 58
Bok choy (Chinese
    white cabbage),
    to grill, 27
    grilled, 61
Bread,
    grilled sandwiches
        of,
        Italian, 49
        Middle Eastern
            flat, 66
        nut, 49
        pita, 66
        rosemary, 49
        rye, 49
    toasted slices, 86
    whole wheat, with
        tempeh, 81
Briquets,
    charcoal, 15, 17
    hardwood, 17
Broccoli,
    to grill, 27
    grilled, 44
Brush, basting, of
    aluminum foil, 16
Brussels sprouts, to
    grill, 27–28
Buckwheat. *See* Kasha
Burdock *(gobo),* to grill,
    28
Butter, for basting, 21,
    53

C

Cabbage,

celery. *See* Napa
    cabbage
Chinese. *See Napa
    cabbage*
white. *See* Bok
    choy
Capers, 76, 79, 90
Carrots,
    to grill, 28
    grilled, 44, 54, 58,
        70, 74
Cauliflower,
    to grill, 28
    grilled, 74
Celeriac (celery knob,
    celery root, turnip-
    rooted celery), to
    grill, 28
Celery,
    knob (root). *See*
        Celeriac
    turnip-rooted. *See*
        Celeriac
Charcoal,
    adding extra, 17–18
    briquets, 15, 17
    hardwood, 17
    to light, 15–17
    mesquite, 17
    to store, 18
    types of, 17
Chayote (mirliton,
    vegetable pear), 35,
    37
    grilled, 50
Cheese,
    blue, grilled
        sandwich of, 49
    chèvre. See Cheese,
        goat
    dry jack, 49, 62
    grilled in grape
        leaves, 62
    Fontina, 90
    goat *(chèvre),* and
        eggplant, in pizza
        topping, 88
    Gouda, sandwich of
        smoked, with
        roasted peppers, 49
    Monterey Jack, in

quesadillas, 50
    mozzarella, 90
    Parmesan, 90
    pecorino, 79
    Swiss, grilled
        sandwich of, with
        red onion, 49
Chili pepper. *See*
    Pepper, chili
Chips, wood, to flavor
    smoke, 18
Chunks, wood, to flavor
    smoke, 18
Cilantro, 50
    sauce, 50
Coals,
    adding extra, 16
    to light extra, 15
    temperature of, 16
Cocktails, grilled
    nibbles for, 86
Coconut milk,
    in marinade, 44
    in sauce, 85
Corn,
    with black beans, 43
    on the cob, grilled,
        50, 53
    to grill, 29
Corn bread, stuffing of,
    65
Corn cakes, with
    roasted vegetables,
    73
Cornmeal, 73
Courgette. *See* Zucchini
Couscous, with fresh
    figs and vegetables,
    54
Cream,
    in sauce, 50, 58
    sour, 73
    sauce of, 83
Curry,
    and ginger sauce, 69
    in *satay,* 85

D

Daikon,

to grill, 29
    grilled, 61
Doneness, determining,
    18
Dressing,
    tahini, 66
    see also Mayonnaise;
        Vinaigrette

E

Eggplant (aubergine),
    to grill, 29
    and goat cheese pizza
        topping, 88
    grilled,
        Japanese, 86
        with new potatoes
            and fennel, 83
        with pasta, 57
    sandwich of, 66
    with tempeh, 81
Eggs,
    in *aïoli,* 69
    hard-boiled, in
        sandwiches, 66, 76
Endive,
    Belgian,
        to grill, 27
        grilled, 70, 86
    curly *(frisée),* in
        salad, 70

F

Fennel (sweet anise),
    to grill, 29
    grilled,
        with new potatoes
            and eggplant, 83
    sandwich of, with
        feta, 49
    in salad, 46
    and tomato pizza
        topping, 90
Figs, fresh, 54
    to grill, 29
    grilled, with
        vegetables and

couscous, 54
Fire,
  to light, 15–17
  to prolong, 16, 17–18
  ready for cooking, 16
Flare-ups, handling, 18
Foccacia, 62
  with grilled yam, 62
Frisée. See Endive, curly, 70
Fruit, to grill, 13
Fuel, mail-order sources of, 91

G

Garam masala, 74
Garlic,
  elephant, 30
  to flavor oil, 21
  to grill, 30
  grilled (roasted) whole, 73, 86
  and mushroom pizza topping, 88
Ginger,
  and curry sauce, 69
  soy, and orange marinade, 61
Gobo. See Burdock
Grape leaves, dry jack cheese in, 62
Grill basket, hinged wire, 16
  using, 44
Grill Book, contents of, 92
Grilling,
  closed, 15
  open, 15
  techniques of, for vegetables, 13–15
  tips for, 17–18
Grills,
  to clean, 18
  to extinguish, 18
  Griffo, 16
  mail-order sources of, 91

H

Hardwood,
  to flavor smoke, 18
  using, 17
Hazelnuts, in rice salad, 46
Heat. *See* Temperature
Herbs, sauce of fresh, 57

J

Jícama (Mexican potato, yam bean),
  to grill, 30–31
  grilled, 50

K

Kasha (buckwheat), 58
Kindling, to start, 15
Kohlrabi (cabbage turnip), to grill, 31

L

Leeks,
  to grill, 31
  grilled, 53, 58
Lemon,
  mayonnaise, sweet, 81
  vinaigrette, 62, 70
Lemongrass, 44
  in marinade, 44
  with tofu, 85
Lighter fluid, 15–16
Lo bok. See Daikon

M

Mail order, for equipment, 91
Mango salsa, 65
Marinade,
  Asian flavors, 19
  coconut, lime, and ginger, 44
  effect of, 18–19
  Italian flavors, 19
  Latin flavors, 19
  pans for, 16
  soy, ginger, and orange, 61
  tangy mustard, 19
  wine, 19, 81
Mayonnaise, sweet lemon, for grilled tempeh, 81
Melon,
  to grill, 31
  tree. *See* Papaya
Mesquite, 17
Mint,
  and parsley sauce, 54
  in salad, 66
Mirliton. See Chayote
Mitts, 17
Mushrooms,
  to grill, 31
  to store, 76

Black Forest. *See* Mushrooms, *shiitake*
Boletus (cèpe, porcini), 31, 54
  browntop. *See* Mushrooms, Crimini
  button (cultivated), 31
  cèpe. See Mushrooms, *Boletus*
  Cremini. *See* Mushrooms, Crimini
  Crimini (browntop, Cremini, Roman), 31
    grilled, with figs, 54
  cultivated. *See* Mushrooms, button
  oyster, 31, 54, 76
    and garlic, in pizza topping, 88
  porcini. See Mushrooms, *Boletus*
  Portobello, 31, 54, 76
    garlicky, 76
  Roman. *See* Mushrooms, Crimini
  shiitake (Black Forest), 31
    grilled, 44, 61
Mustard, Dijon-style, in marinade, 19
Mustard greens,
  to grill, 32
  sauce of, 58

N

Nam pla, 44, 85
  in marinade, 44
  in sauce, 85
Napa cabbage (celery cabbage, Chinese cabbage), to grill, 32
Newspapers, as kindling, 15
Noodles, silver, with basil, 44
Nuts,
  almonds, sauce of spicy, 74
  pecan,
    in corn-bread stuffing, 65
    spicy butter (sauce)

of, 53
pine, in polenta, 79

O

Oil,
  canola, 21
  flavor-infused, to make, 21
  for grilling, 21
  nut, 13, 21
  olive, 13, 21
  peanut, 19, 21
  safflower, 21
  sesame, 19
Okra, to grill, 32
Olives,
  and tomato, in pizza topping, 90
  types of, 86
Onions,
  to grill, 32–33
  green (spring),
    to grill, 30
    grilled, 44, 73
  red,
    grilled, 43, 50
    in sandwiches, 49, 66
    with tempeh, 81
  spring. *See* Onions, green
  torpedo, grilled, 58
Orange juice,
  in marinade, 19, 61
  and sour cream sauce, 73
  in vinaigrette, 69
Oranges, in salad, 46

P

Pan, for marinading, 16
Papaya (pawpaw, tree melon), to grill, 33
Pappadums, 74
Parsley,
  and mint sauce, 54
  in salsa, 79
  in spaghetti sauce, 76
Parsnips,
  to grill, 33
  grilled, 58
Pasta,
  with fresh herb sauce and grilled vegetables, 57
  shells, 57
  spaghetti, with piquant green sauce and mushrooms, 76

Pattypan (scaloppini, scallop squash), 37
Pawpaw. *See* Papaya
Pea, sugar (snow pea), to grill, 37–38
Peach, to grill, 33
Peanuts, in sauce, 85
Pear,
  to grill, 33
  vegetable. *See* Chayote
Peel, citrus, to flavor smoke, 18
Pepper,
  to blacken, 49
  chili,
    described, 33–34
    to grill, 34
    Anaheim, 33, 43
    ancho, 34
    banana (Hungarian Wax), 33, 43
    chilaca. See Pepper, chili, *pasilla*
    chipotle, 65
    sauce of, 65
    Hungarian Wax. *See* Pepper, chili, banana
    jalapeño, 21, 43
    pasilla (chilaca), 33
    poblano, 34
  sweet bell,
    to grill, 34
    corn bread-stuffed, 65
    grilled, 49, 50, 70, 73
    in polenta, 43
    roasted, 49
Pineapple,
  to grill, 34–65
  grilled, in salad, 70
Pizza, wood-smoked, 88–90
Plantain. *See* Banana
Polenta,
  basil and pine nut, 79
  with green chili and red pepper, 43
  sauce for, 76
Pomegranates, in salsa, 65
Poppyseed, and orange vinaigrette, 69
Potatoes,
  to grill, 35
  grilled, 58, 74
  new, grilled, 70, 83
  sweet. *See* Sweet potato

Vegetables on the Grill

Q

Quesadillas, with avocado and jack cheese, 50
Quinoa, 70
   summer salad of, 70

R

Radicchio, to grill, 35
Radish, Japanese. *See* Daikon
Rice,
   basmati, 74
   brown, 69
   three-grain, 69
   Wehani, 69
   wild. *See* Wild rice
Rutabaga (Swedish turnip), to grill, 35
Rye, berries, 69

S

Salad,
   avocado and papaya, 43
   mixed greens and sorrel, 53
   oranges and fennel, 46
   summer, with quinoa, 70
   tangerine, green onion, and mint, 66
Salsa,
   cruda, for polenta, 79
   mango, 65
Sandwiches, grilled, 49, 66
   blue cheese, 49
   feta cheese and fennel, 49
   Middle Eastern eggplant, with tahini, 66
   smoked Gouda and peppers, 49
   Swiss cheese and red onion, 49
Satay, 85
   sauce, 85
   tofu, 85
Sauce,
   adobo, 65
   aïoli, 69
   basting, 21, 53
   chipotle, for stuffed peppers, 65
   cilantro, for grilled vegetables, 50
   curry-ginger, for grilled vegetables, 69
   fish. *See Nam pla*
   fresh herb, for grilled vegetables, 57
   hoisin, in basting sauce, 21
   mustard greens, for grilled root vegetables, 58
   Northern Indian almond-spice, for grilled vegetables, 74
   orange cream, for corn cakes and roasted vegetables, 73
   parsley-mint, for grilled figs and vegetables, 54
   piquant green, for spaghetti, 76
   satay, 85
   sour cream, for eggplant, new potatoes, and fennel, 83
   soy, 19
   spicy pecan nut, 53
   tangy dipping, 85
   see also Salsa; Vinaigrette
Scallion. *See* Onion, green
Scaloppini. *See* Squash, pattypan
Shallots,
   to grill, 35
   grilled, 54
Skewers, 17, 44, 58
Smoke, to flavor, 18
Sorrel, 53, 66
Soy sauce, in marinade, 61
Spaghetti. *See* Pasta
Spatula (turner), 17
Spinach, in salad, 70
Squash,
   acorn (table queen), 37
   roasted, with wild rice salad, 46
   banana, 37
   buttercup, 37
   butternut, 37
   crookneck (yellow), 35, 37
   grilled, in salad, 70
   delicata (sweet potato squash), 37
   Hubbard, 37
   kabocha, 37
   pattypan (scallop, scaloppini), grilled, 50, 57, 70, 73
   scallop. *See* Squash, pattypan
   scaloppini. *See* Squash, pattypan
   summer, 35, 37
   to grill, 37
   grilled, with pasta, 57
   sweet potato. *See* Squash, delicata
   table queen. *See* Squash, acorn
   winter,
   described, 37
   to grill, 37
   grilled, 74
   yellow. *See* Squash, crookneck
Starter,
   charcoal, 15
   charcoal chimney, 15
   electric coil, 15
   solid, 16
Stuffing, corn-bread, 65
Sunchoke. *See* Artichoke, Jerusalem
Sunroot. *See* Artichoke, Jerusalem
Sweet potato,
   to grill, 38
   grilled, 58

T

Tahini, dressing for grilled sandwich, 66
Tempeh, 81
   to grill, 38
   grilled, with red onion and eggplant, 81
Temperature, to control, 15, 16, 18
Time, required to grill vegetables, 15
Tofu (bean curd),
   to grill, 38
   mushrooms, daikon, and bok choy, grilled, 61
   satay, with tangy dipping sauce, 85
Tomate verde. See Tomatillo
Tomatillo (Mexican green tomato, *tomate verde*), to grill, 39
Tomatoes,
   to grill, 39
   grilled, 44
   to peel, 79
   and fennel pizza topping, 90
   cherry,
   grilled, 50, 62
   in salad, 70
   Mexican green. *See* Tomatillo
   pear, grilled, with pasta, 57
   sun-dried,
   and olive pizza topping, 90
   to reconstitute, 90
Tongs, 17
Tools for grilling, 16–17
   mail-order sources of, 91
Topping, pizza, 88–90
   eggplant and goat cheese, 88
   fennel and tomato, 90
   garlic and mushroom, 88
   sun-dried tomato and olive, 90
Tortillas, for *quesadillas,* 50
Turner, *See* Spatula
Turnip,
   to grill, 39
   grilled, 58
   cabbage. *See* Kohlrabi
   Swedish. *See* Rutabaga

V

Vegetables,
   baby, grilled, with pasta and fresh herb sauce, 57
   coconut-lime-and-ginger-marinated, 44
   to grill, 13, 15
   grilled, 57, 58
   with almond-spice sauce, 74
   with cilantro sauce, 50
   with dipping sauces, 69
   with fennel sauce, 50
   with fresh figs and couscous, 54
   roasted, with corn cakes, 73
   root, with warm mustard greens sauce, 58
   salad of grilled, 70
   sauce for grilled, 76
Vermicelli, rice, 44
Vinaigrette,
   creamy lemon, for asparagus, 62
   lemon-mustard, for grilled vegetable salad, 70
   poppyseed-orange, 69
Vinegar, balsamic, in marinade, 19

W

Watercress, in salsa, 65, 66
Wheat, berries, 69
Wild rice, salad of, 46
Wine, marinade of, 19, 81
Wood,
   mesquite, 17
   types of, to flavor smoke, 18

Y

Yams,
   apples, and leeks, with spicy pecan nut butter, 53
   to grill, 39
   grilled, 58, 62
Yogurt, in sauce, 54, 65, 69, 74

Z

Zucchini (courgette), 37
   grilled, 44, 50, 54, 57, 70, 73